ESSAY ON THE FREEDOM OF THE WILL

Essay on the
Freedom of the Will

Arthur Schopenhauer

Translated with an Introduction by
Konstantin Kolenda

DOVER PUBLICATIONS
Garden City, New York

DOVER PHILOSOPHICAL CLASSICS

Bibliographical Note

This Dover edition, first published in 2005, is an unabridged republication of the translation originally published, as part of The Library of Liberal Arts, by the Bobbs-Merrill Company, Inc., Indianapolis and New York, in 1960. Schopenhauer's essay originally appeared in German as "Über die Freiheit des menschlichen Willens" in his book *Die beiden Grundprobleme der Ethik* (The Two Fundamental Problems of Ethics), which was first published by Joh. Christ. Hermannsche Buchhandlung, Frankfurt am Main, in 1841. The other half of that book was Schopenhauer's essay "Über das Fundament der Moral" (On the Basis of Morality).

Library of Congress Cataloging-in-Publication Data

Schopenhauer, Arthur, 1788-1860.
    [Über die Freiheit des menschlichen Willens. English]
    Essay on the freedom of the will / Arthur Schopenhauer ; translated, with an introduction, by Konstantin Kolenda.
      p. cm. — (Dover philosophical classics)
    Originally published: Indianapolis : Bobbs-Merrill, 1960. (The library of liberal arts)
    Includes bibliographical references (p.   ).
    ISBN-13: 978-0-486-44011-8 (pbk.)
    ISBN-10: 0-486-44011-7 (pbk.)
    1. Free will and determinism. I. Kolenda, Konstantin. II. Title. III. Series.

B3144.U352E5 2005
123'.5—dc22

                 2004061899

Printed in the United States of America
44011709   2022
www.doverpublications.com

CONTENTS

· · · · · · · · · · · · · · · · ·

ESSAY ON THE
FREEDOM OF THE WILL

INTRODUCTION

Twenty years after the publication of the first edition of his main work, *The World as Will and Idea,* Schopenhauer submitted his prize essay *On the Freedom of the Will* to the Norwegian Scientific Society. While this essay won the offered prize in 1839, Schopenhauer's second contribution to the subject of ethics, *The Foundation of Morality,* was denied the prize of the Royal Danish Academy of Sciences in 1840. In the following year Schopenhauer published both essays together under the title *The Two Fundamental Problems of Ethics,* not failing to indicate in the subtitles how the essays fared at the hands of the respective Societies. Ironically, the one which was refused the prize of the Danish Academy was translated into English (by A. B. Bullock, London, 1903), while the essay on the freedom of the will has so far not been available to English readers.

One may look at this essay in two ways. It can be used as an introduction to Schopenhauer's philosophy in general. His treatment of the problem of free will, a problem regarded by him as one of the most important in modern philosophy, reveals many basic features of his thought. To show this, some references to his main work will be necessary. On the other hand, Schopenhauer's essay admits of being studied independently of his metaphysical views. What he has to say on the subject is by no means obsolete. On the contrary, recent revival of interest in the notion of will makes it desirable to examine Schopenhauer's penetrating reflections in this area.

I

Schopenhauer fully accepted the consequences of Kant's "Copernican revolution": knowledge is conditioned by the a priori forms which the knowing subject imposes on experience. The very first line of his main work, "The world is my idea," is a paraphrase of Kant's conclusion that mind makes nature possible. Schopenhauer draws further inferences from this conclusion. The world as idea does not appear as it ultimately is. While Kant admitted this and pointed to the thing-in-itself as the unknowable "other side" of appearances, Schopenhauer believed that we actually do have access to this other side. "The objective world, the world as idea, is not the only side of the world, but merely its outward side; and it has an entirely different side—the side of its inmost nature—its kernel—the thing-in-itself." [1] And what is this kernel, the thing-in-itself? "The answer to the riddle is given to the subject of knowledge who appears as an individual, and the answer is *will*." [2] Every act of the body becomes objectification of will by passing into perception. Thus man is in possession of double knowledge of the nature and activity of his body: as idea and as will.

Schopenhauer now takes a further step. He uses this double knowledge of ourselves as "a key to the nature of every phenomenon in nature," and concludes that *all* bodies are analogous to ours in this respect. In its inner nature every being and every object must be "the same as that in us which we call *will*." Schopenhauer justifies this step by saying that "besides will and idea nothing is known to us or thinkable." [3] Like Whitehead in our times, he sees no reason why we should not use human experience as providing a clue to the character of all entities in the world.

The will is one, eternal, indestructible, almighty. The principle of multiplicity and individuation does not apply to the will itself, but only to its manifestations. They take place in time and space, and are subject without exception to the law of causality. However, Schopenhauer insists that the thing-in-itself, or will, "is present entire and undivided in every object

---

[1] Arthur Schopenhauer, *The World as Will and Idea*, I, 39, trans. Haldane and Kemp. Hereafter referred to as *WWI*. Quotations are taken from this translation.

[2] *Ibid.*, p. 129.   [3] *Ibid.*, p. 136.

of nature and in every living being." [4] Will is the same in all beings and is indestructible. Accordingly, the destruction of one real being, including its inner nature or will, would be equivalent to the destruction of the whole world.[5]

The world is the objectification of will. All manifestations of will reveal its character: it is at variance, indeed at war, with itself. Schopenhauer is impressed by the ubiquity of strife and conflict on all levels of existence. "Every grade of the objectification of will fights for the matter, the space and the time of the others," [6] and this is true of all phenomena: mechanical, physical, chemical, organic, human. Although manifesting the same will, all phenomena and beings in nature express different original powers, and Schopenhauer distinguished between various grades of the objectification of will.[7] He describes the differences among these original powers in terms of various forms of causality.[8] To each type of original power there corresponds a type of causality, so that these types can be used to distinguish between various grades of the objectified will. Cause in the narrowest sense operates within the realm of inorganic, physicochemical phenomena: stimulus in the realm of plant life, and motivation in the life of animals, including man. Although motivation is the type of causality which operates in all animals, men are also in possession of abstract reason; this distinguishes them from all other animals which can react only to perceptual cognition.[9]

In *The World as Will and Idea* Schopenhauer introduces also the concept of Platonic Idea. Although the function of this concept in the system is not very clear, Schopenhauer seems to use it as expressing the form of various objectifications of will. Platonic Idea appears to be that aspect in the original power which is open to cognitive grasp by a knowing

---

4 *Ibid.*, p. 168.   5 *Ibid.*, p. 167.

6 *Ibid.*, p. 191.   7 *Ibid.*, p. 166.

8 *Ibid.*, pp. 202-4. See also chap. III of this work.

9 S. K. Langer in her book, *Philosophy in a New Key* (Cambridge, Mass.: 1942), makes a similar distinction by differentiating between signs and symbols.

subject. But it is not a mere concept; like Plato, Schopenhauer wanted to preserve also the dynamic aspect of Ideas.[10]

We are further told that the will always seeks the highest possible objectification.[11] The clearest and fullest objectification of will is man as Platonic Idea.[12] But this does not mean that will is not interested in objectifying itself in other possible ways. The presence of other organisms and inorganic bodies in the world shows that they are also necessary for a complete objectification of will.[13] What is of greatest interest, however, is that Schopenhauer views the objectification of will in human existence as a creative frontier of universal will. Unlike Plato, he does not postulate the existence of an Idea of humanity to which every particular human being tries to approximate. This is the case only within the realm of plants and lower animals. In these grades of the objectification of will, to know the Idea of the species is to know how each individual animal will behave. But not so in regard to men. To know the objectification of will in a man we do need to know some things about the human species in general, but this is far from sufficient. To know the will as it manifests itself either in our own person or in others, we must study and try to fathom each special individual and personal character.[14] This implies that human beings cannot be reduced to mere types. Personal character expresses itself by "giving prominence to a particular side of the Idea of humanity. . . . No individual and no action can be without significance; in all and through all the Idea of man unfolds itself more and more." [15] This is an important feature of Schopenhauer's philosophy. His insistence on the irreducibility of the human person may provide a foil against which the contemporary tendency to explain the self wholly in terms of environment and conditioning may be better appraised. Schopenhauer's view on this matter is diametrically opposed to the behavioristic interpretation of man, in which even the meaningfulness of

10 *WWI*, pp. 226, 303.   11 *Ibid.*, p. 190.
12 *Ibid.*, p. 200.   13 *Ibid.*, p. 200.
14 *Ibid.*, p. 170.   15 *Ibid.*, p. 297.

the concept of personality is questioned. Undoubtedly Schopenhauer's general view has in it many serious, perhaps insur-
mountable difficulties. Nevertheless, it represents a strong
alternative to the modern tendency to explain the idea of a
human person by explaining it away.

Schopenhauer believed that his metaphysical insights bear
moral fruits: they provide the unique objectifications of will
—human persons—with the understanding both of their own
inner nature and of the basic character of universal will. This
knowledge can be *used* by each particular human objectification of will. A startling and most difficult point in Schopenhauer's whole system (a point to which I shall return later on),
is that the individual will can use this knowledge to turn itself against the universal will of which it is a manifestation.
Knowledge of the nature of all objectified will may lead each
individual to seek experiences in which this will is made
quiescent and lured away from its inevitable bent for ceaseless
striving. Two types of experience provide such liberation from
the pangs of the will: creation and appreciation of great art,
and compassion for the suffering of others. Art gives knowledge of Platonic Ideas and this knowledge reduces the effectiveness of particular perceptions as motives and thus quiets
the will.[16] The breaking free from the bondage to the will
occurs even more fully and radically when a knowing subject
recognizes himself *and* others as manifestations of the same
will. Seeing that suffering is a necessary concomitant of will's
activity, such a subject will express his liberation through
sympathy, compassion.[17]

The nature of the moral fruits which Schopenhauer claims
to reap from his metaphysical insights has puzzled many a
reader, even though it is presented with the full force of the
philosopher's conviction and eloquence. At the center of
Schopenhauer's argument, however, stands the notion of
freedom. Like Kant, he thinks of human freedom as tran-

16 *Ibid.*, pp. 254-56, 367.

17 *Ibid.*, pp. 458, 478. Cf. also T. B. Saunders (trans.), *Complete Essays
of Schopenhauer* (New York: 1942), Book VI, 96.

scendental, or as independent of the principle of sufficient reason. It is this freedom that makes it possible for man to turn against himself as a phenomenon, provided that he has grasped the nature of his own will and of will in general. Thus freedom seems to stand in a definite relation to philosophic knowledge. For this reason, Schopenhauer's views on freedom are extremely important for his whole system and can serve as a test and touchstone of his final conclusions.

II

The argument of the essay is clearly and vigorously presented and need not be anticipated here. Most briefly, Schopenhauer believed that the traditional defenders of the freedom of the will actually argued in favor of indeterminism, and this he rejects. To accept indeterminism is to relegate actions to absolute chance. Not only is this inconceivable, but it also eliminates the ground for moral responsibility. Most ethical theorists today similarly reject indeterminism, and for the same reason. But freedom of the will need not be identified with indeterminism, for determinism and freedom of the will are not mutually exclusive. Philosophers today seem to accept the view that freedom of the will is not only compatible with determinism, but also requires it.[18] Schopenhauer also combines determinism and freedom, but what is unique about his way of doing this is that he ascribes freedom to the character of man. Character is freely assumed by every human being, and this is why we feel morally responsible for our behavior. The final chapter of the essay contains a detailed statement of Schopenhauer's views on this point.

The peculiar feature of motivation as a type of causality is that in it two factors operate simultaneously: the given motive and the given character. First of all, are motives causes? There seems to be no harm in saying this, especially when one makes clear that by a "cause" is meant nothing more

[18] Cf. R. B. Hobart, "Free Will as Involving Determination and Inconceivable Without It," *Mind* (1934).

than a "determining ground," and goes on to describe in detail what kind of determining ground a motive is. Schopenhauer does this. He makes it clear that a motive, in human behavior, may be no more than a mere thought, hence something abstract and immaterial. But it must be a thought which can have influence on the will of the man who thinks it. Given this condition, and in the absence of possible counter-motives, Schopenhauer tells us that the man is bound to act on the motive which affects his will. By itself the motive is powerless, but when it acts on a proper will the action suggested by the motive will necessarily follow.

The character of a man, consequently, is always one of the causes which bring about actions. But what kind of cause is character? What do we know about its nature? Nothing at all. It is on a par with all other original powers in nature, hence inexplicable. Thus if character is one of the causal factors in the performance of actions, *it* is absolutely free. Yet it is not free with respect to the motive which acts on it. Being what it is, the character *must* respond to the motive. Schopenhauer claims that the entire conduct of a man is determined by the free volition of his timeless, inborn, and unchangeable character.[19] This makes it a priori impossible for a character to change in time. In order to will differently in given circumstances an agent would have to become another person, but this Schopenhauer considers impossible.[20]

III

Two questions arise at this point: 1) Is it intelligible to speak of the timeless character as one of the causes of every particular action performed by the person who has this character? 2) What does it mean to say that a person has an inborn, unchangeable character?

We must answer the first question in the negative because it is confusing, if not self-contradictory, to speak of something which is *outside* of time as *causing* something which is

[19] *WWI*, pp. 372-3.   [20] *Ibid.*, p. 147.

in time. Schopenhauer himself insisted that the principle of causality is applicable only within the world of space and time, and yet in this instance he speaks of causality as describing the relation between the timeless and the temporal. He cannot have it both ways. Moreover, to put a temporal action in a relation to something which is inexplicable does not throw any light either on the action or on that which remains inexplicable. (In one instance Schopenhauer expressed dissatisfaction with the fact that the timeless character is groundless and admits only of a transcendental explanation, which is really no explanation at all. His essay on Character ends with this sentence: "Perhaps some one will come after me who will throw light into this dark abyss." [21])

The way in which Schopenhauer answers the second question involves him in a similar difficulty. He claims that by seeing how we act we find out *what we are*. By the phrase "what we are" he apparently means more than our empirical character; it includes the real being or essence of our selves. But what do we know about this real essence? There is only one way of answering this question: we must examine the motives to which each particular character responds. But if so, the informative value of the phrase "our actions proceed from our character" is deceptive. What do we find out when we see ourselves responding repeatedly to a certain motive? No more than that we are the sort of person who repeatedly responds to that kind of motive. We do not find out anything which is timeless and unchangeable in our character.

Furthermore, if by seeing how we act we find out what we are, there must be some correspondence between our empirical and our timeless characters. So a change in conduct may be an indication that the real character of a man is at least ambivalent and capable of change. Schopenhauer does not admit this. "The conduct of a man may be observedly changed without justifying us in concluding that his character has been changed." [22] How does Schopenhauer know this?

21 *Complete Essays,* Book VI, 85.
22 *WWI,* p. 379.

The only evidence he *can* have is the changes in observable conduct, and this evidence seems to go against his view.

In the light of these considerations, Schopenhauer's claim that character is inborn and unchangeable becomes quite dubious. The only support which he provides for this contention is that most people are to some degree consistent in responding to certain motives, and that some men show a very high degree of such consistency. Schopenhauer's examples come from the extreme ends of the scale: saints, on the one hand, and hardened criminals, on the other. But it seems that in choosing these examples he was trying hard to fit the facts to his theory.

In spite of this unsupportable a priori view of character, Schopenhauer sees clearly that the concepts of freedom and responsibility are both attributable to *persons* and that blame and praise are possible because we recognize ourselves as agents of our acts. This is a sound part of his doctrine. But he is probably mistaken in claiming that we feel responsible for our character. We feel responsible for it only to the extent that we had a hand in forming it, and this is a matter of having done some things and having left other things undone in our past. Schopenhauer himself recognizes that self-knowledge is important and involves self-acceptance. He describes a person of acquired character as the one who has the most perfect knowledge possible of his individuality.[23] In doing this, however, he tends to underestimate the place of knowledge in human action. Here we touch on another central issue in ethics, namely the problem of the relation between will and reason. Schopenhauer's treatment of it deserves further discussion.

Ostensibly, Schopenhauer views the function of reason as purely instrumental. "Will is first and original; knowledge is merely added to it as an instrument belonging to the phenomenon of will."[24] The most that reason can do is to preserve resolutions which have been made, to provide maxims to

23 *Ibid.*, pp. 393, 394, 396.
24 *Ibid.*, p. 377. Cf. also p. 113.

withstand a weakness of the moment, and to give consistency to action.[25] Schopenhauer rightly points out that if we must say that knowledge of objects is *interesting,* then we must admit that it is in some way related to our will. As Kant would say, even a disinterested quest of knowledge, although it does not stem *from* interest, may nevertheless be pursued because we take interest in it. Hence, the uses of reason are *uses* and satisfy human needs, even though among these needs may be a mere desire to understand.

Like Hume, Schopenhauer says that the intellect is capable only of unfolding possible motives; otherwise it is passive.[26] Only the will is active. But as indicated above, the most peculiar feature of human motivation, or causality mediated through cognition, is that, though subordinated to the service of the will, it can oppose that very will. It should not escape our notice that to some extent this begins to happen at the level of mere abstract thought. Even though abstract ideas, according to Schopenhauer, are still in the service of the will and are used by it primarily as motives, the perceiving and thinking individual sometimes becomes a pure subject of knowledge and is not dominated by the perceptual present. When the subject rises from the knowledge of individual objects to the knowledge of Ideas, he is liberated from the bondage of will.

This ability of will to turn against itself through intellectual grasp of the nature of reality is itself a kind of mystery and raises the question whether reason for Schopenhauer is indeed merely instrumental, as he seems to have claimed. It seems that the liberation from the domination of the will begins as soon as an organism becomes capable of abstract thought.[27] For then it is no longer in the clutches of the perceptual present, and its character has a range of possible choices which is as large as the scope of its abstract ideas. If we remember that the free will reveals itself in its tendency to respond to some motives, we shall see that the extent of its freedom will

25 *Ibid.,* p. 75.   26 *Ibid.,* pp. 376, 378.
27 *Ibid.,* p. 230.

be proportionate to the scope of motives to which it may respond. The necessary condition for a will to respond to a motive is that it be aware of this motive. The freedom of the will is virtually restricted by ignorance of the particular subject in which will manifests itself. Conversely, the greater the scope of possible motives (i.e., the greater the intelligence and knowledge) the freer the will. Thus, for Schopenhauer, as for Spinoza, all our freedom is in our thought. Contemplation of ideas in art, and compassionate acceptance of other persons, are the final fruits of seeing things in their timeless character, *sub specie aeternitatis*.[28]

Although Schopenhauer insisted that virtue, like genius, cannot be taught,[29] he left no doubt that enlightenment of the will is morally desirable and effective. "The character itself may be completely suppressed or abolished through the change of knowledge referred to above." [30] In the light of this admission, the insistence on the unchangeability of character is harmless indeed and may merely testify to Schopenhauer's predilection for a pessimistic view of human nature. If we do not know what the unchanging ends of a person are except by means of what he actually pursues in particular situations, how can we say that these ends remain unchanged even though the pursued ends do change? If rational persuasion can induce a man to realize the end of possessing certain things not by stealing them but by working for them, are we not entitled to speak of a real change in this man's character? In this case the ends *are* affected by the change of means, and this change may have been brought about by a change in this man's knowledge.[31]

At least in one instance Schopenhauer admitted that reason can have direct influence on the will. He said that reason

---

[28] *Complete Essays,* Book VI, pp. 75-78.

[29] *WWI,* pp. 349-50.   [30] *Ibid.,* p. 521.

[31] This criticism is applicable also to Kant's view of man as end-in-himself, in distinction from various ends which men may pursue. For an excellent discussion of this topic see M. G. Singer, "The Categorical Imperative," *Philosophical Review,* LXIII, 4 (October, 1954), pp. 577-591.

disturbs the empirical expression of the irrational character by always keeping before it "what becomes man in general." [32] Here Schopenhauer acknowledges the formative influence of reflection. It is by holding up to a man the possibilities open to man in general that the intellect participates directly in developing capacities and powers which otherwise would never have come to the surface. Herein lies the value of instruction and education. Thus, if the irrational will can be at least disturbed by considerations of reason, it cannot be completely irrational.

Schopenhauer thought of himself as a teacher of mankind. In this capacity he sometimes resorted to outright moral exhortation. Because our actions are the mirror of our timeless will and we get to know ourselves after the actions took place, "It behooves us to strive and fight in time, in order that the picture we produce by our deeds may be such that the contemplation of it may calm us as much as possible instead of harassing us." [33] Here speaks a philosopher who earnestly believes in the efficacy of moral effort and knows that his effort can have a measure of success only if it is enlightened. He urges men to find this enlightenment in self-knowledge, in the awareness of what is possible for man by studying human culture and history, in the appreciation of great works of art, and in the acts of compassion toward all who suffer.

In conclusion I wish to acknowledge my indebtedness to my colleagues, Professor R. A. Tsanoff and Professor J. S. Fulton. This translation would not have been without their urging and encouragement.

I also thank Professor B. Q. Morgan, Professor Ernst F. Winter, and the General Editor of this series, Mr. Oskar Piest, for their numerous suggestions and improvements of style. Professor Morgan and Mrs. J. S. Fulton have contributed new translations of poetry quoted by Schopenhauer, which I gratefully acknowledge.

KONSTANTIN KOLENDA

[32] *WWI*, p. 391.   [33] *Ibid.*, p. 390.

SELECTED BIBLIOGRAPHY

I. Collected Works

Schopenhauers sämtliche Werke.
Edited by Paul Deussen. München, 1911-ff. 15 vols.
Schopenhauers sämtliche Werke.
Edited by Eduard Grisebach. Leipzig, 1892. 6 vols.
Schopenhauers sämtliche Werke.
Edited by Julius Frauenstädt. Leipzig, 1873-4.

II. Translations

The World as Will and Idea, by R. B. Haldane and J. Kemp. London, 1907-09.
On the Fourfold Root of the Principle of Sufficient Reason and on the Will in Nature, by Mme. K. Hillebrand. London, 1888.
The Basis of Morality, by A. B. Bullock. London, 1903.
Religion and Other Essays, by T. B. Saunders. London, 1910.
Selected Essays of Arthur Schopenhauer, by E. B. Bax. London, 1912.
Counsels and Maxims, by T. B. Saunders. London, 1890.
The Art of Literature, by T. B. Saunders. London, 1891.
The Art of Controversy, by T. B. Saunders. New York, 1896.
The Wisdom of Life, by T. B. Saunders. London, 1902.
Complete Essays of Schopenhauer, by T. B. Saunders. New York, 1942.
Philosophy of Arthur Schopenhauer, by E. B. Bax and T. B. Saunders. New York, 1933.
The Works of Schopenhauer, abridged and edited by Will Durant. New York, 1933.
The Philosophy of Schopenhauer, edited by Irvin Edman. New York, 1928.
The Living Thoughts of Schopenhauer, presented by Thomas Mann. New York, 1939.

III. Works on Schopenhauer in German

Busch, H., *Das Testament Arthur Schopenhauers*. Wiesbaden, 1950.

Fischer, Kuno, *Schopenhauers Leben, Werke und Lehre*. Heidelberg, 1898.

Grisebach, Eduard, *Schopenhauer, Neue Beiträge zur Geschichte seines Lebens*. Berlin, 1905.

Gwinner, Wilhelm, *Schopenhauers Leben*. Leipzig, 1878.

Lessing, Theodor, *Schopenhauer, Wagner, Nietzsche*. München, 1906.

Nietzsche, Friedrich, *Schopenhauer als Erzieher* (third part of *Unzeitgemässe Betrachtungen, Nietzsches Werke*. Leipzig, 1917, vol. I).

Paulsen, Friedrich, *Schopenhauer, Hamlet, Mephistopheles*. Berlin, 1905.

Simmel, Georg, *Schopenhauer und Nietzsche*. Leipzig, 1907.

Volkelt, J. I., *Arthur Schopenhauer*. Stuttgart, 1900.

Zint, H., *Schopenhauer als Erlebnis*. München, 1954.

IV. Works on Schopenhauer in English

Caldwell, W., *Schopenhauer's System in Its Philosophical Significance*. Edinburgh, 1896.

Colvin, S. S., *Schopenhauer's Doctrine of the Thing-in-Itself*. Providence, 1897.

Copleston, Frederick, *Arthur Schopenhauer, Philosopher of Pessimism*. London, 1947.

McGill, V. J., *Schopenhauer, Pessimist and Pagan*. New York, 1931.

Tsanoff, R. A., *Schopenhauer's Criticism of Kant's Theory of Experience*. New York, 1911.

Wallace, William, *Life of Arthur Schopenhauer*. London, 1890.

Whittaker, Thomas, *Schopenhauer*. London, 1909.

Zimmern, Helen, *Arthur Schopenhauer, His Life and His Philosophy*. London, 1876.

ESSAY ON THE
FREEDOM OF THE WILL

ESSAY ON THE FREEDOM OF THE WILL

～⚜ I ⚜～

DEFINITION OF CONCEPTS

A question which is so important, serious, and difficult, and which coincides in essentials with a basic problem of the entire philosophy of medieval and modern times, needs to be treated with great precision. An analysis, therefore, of the basic concepts which the question contains is certainly in order.

1) What is freedom?

When carefully examined, this concept turns out to be negative. It signifies merely the absence of any hindrance and restraint. But this restraint, as it manifests power, must be positive. Corresponding to the possible nature of this restraint, the concept has three very different subspecies: physical, intellectual, and moral freedom.

a) *Physical freedom* is the absence of material hindrances of any sort. Thus we say: a clear sky, an open view, clear air, an open field, a vacant place,[1] free heat (which is not bound chemically), free electric charge, free flow of the stream where it is no longer checked by mountains or sluices, etc. Even such expressions as "free room and board," "free press," "post-free letter," signify the absence of those encumbering conditions which often attach themselves to such things and hinder their enjoyment. Most frequently, however, we conceive of freedom as an attribute of animate beings, whose distinctive feature is the ability to originate movements from their own will, that is, voluntarily. Thus such movements are called free when no

1 [The English words: *clear, open, vacant* are rendered in German by the word *frei* (free).—Tr.]

3

material obstacles prevent them. Since these obstacles may be of very different kinds, but that with which they interfere is always the will, for the sake of simplicity one prefers to think of the concept of freedom in positive terms; the concept is used to cover everything that moves or acts only from its own will. This reversal of the concept changes nothing in essentials. Accordingly, in this physical meaning of the concept of freedom, animals and men are called free when their actions are not hindered by any physical or material obstacles—such as fetters, or prison, or paralysis—but proceed in accordance with their will.

This physical meaning of the concept of freedom, especially when predicated on animate beings, is the original, immediate, and hence most frequent one. As such, the concept in this meaning is not subject to doubt or controversy, and its reality can always be authenticated empirically. For whenever an animate being acts only from its will, it is, in the physical sense, free. Here we do not take into account whatever may influence the will itself. For in its original, immediate, and therefore popular meaning, the concept of freedom refers only to the ability to act, that is, precisely to the absence of physical obstacles to its actions. Hence one says: free is the bird in the sky, the wild beast in the forest; man is by nature free; only the free are happy. We also call a nation free, meaning thereby that it is governed solely by laws, but that it has given itself these laws: for in that case it merely obeys its own will. Therefore, political freedom must be included under physical freedom.

However, as soon as we leave physical freedom and consider the two remaining kinds, we are no longer dealing with the popular but with a philosophical sense of the concept. This, as is well known, leads to many difficulties. It falls into two entirely different classes: intellectual and moral freedom.

b) *Intellectual freedom*, "the voluntary and involuntary with respect to thought" [2] in Aristotle, is mentioned here only

---

[2] [Aristotle, *The Works of Aristotle* (Oxford, 1915), IX, *Ethica Eudemia*, Book II, sec. 7, 1223a, 23-25, ed. W. D. Ross.—Tr.]

for the sake of completeness of classification. I shall therefore take the liberty of postponing its discussion to the very end of this essay, when the concepts to be used in it will have been explained in the foregoing sections. This will enable us to deal with intellectual freedom quite concisely. But since it is most closely related to physical freedom, it must follow it in the classification.

c) So I turn directly to the third kind, namely to *moral freedom*. This is really the *liberum arbitrium* cited in the question of the Royal Society. This concept connects with that of physical freedom in a way which makes its necessarily much later origination understandable. Physical freedom, as noted above, has to do only with material obstacles; it is at once present when they are absent. But in some cases it has been observed that a man, without being hindered by material obstacles, was restrained by mere motives—such as threats, promises, dangers, and the like—from acting in a way which, if these motives were absent, would have certainly expressed his will. Consequently, the question was raised whether such a man was still free, or whether the actions which express his actual will could really be checked and prevented just as effectively by a strong countermotive as by a physical obstacle. A sound mind would find no difficulty in arriving at the answer: a motive can never act in the same ways as a physical obstacle. Undoubtedly the latter easily transcends human bodily powers unconditionally, while a motive can never be irresistible in itself and has no absolute power but can be always offset by a stronger countermotive, provided that such a countermotive is present and that the particular man can be determined by it. We often observe that even the strongest of all motives—to preserve one's life—is outweighed by other motives, for example, in suicide or in sacrificing one's life for others, for one's convictions, and for various causes. Conversely, all degrees of the most refined tortures on the rack have now and again been overcome by the mere thought that otherwise life would be lost. But even though it were evident from this that the motives bring with them no purely objective and absolute compulsion, still one could ascribe to them a subjective and relative compulsion: namely, relative to the person involved. In either case the result is the same. Hence the question remains: is the will itself free?

The concept of freedom, until now conceived only in respect to *ability*, was thus put in a relation to *willing*, and so the problem arose whether the willing itself is free. But on close inspection, the original, purely empirical, and hence popular concept of freedom shows itself incapable of becoming thus related to willing. For according to it "free" means "in accordance with one's own will." Consequently, to ask whether the will itself is free, is to ask whether the will is in accordance with itself. This, of course, is self-evident, but says also nothing at all. The empirical concept of freedom signifies: "I am free when I can *do what I will*." Here in the phrase "what I will" the freedom is already affirmed. But when we now inquire about the freedom of willing itself, the question would then take this form: "Can you also will your volitions?", as if a volition depended on another volition which lay behind it. Suppose that this question is answered in the affirmative, what then? Another question would arise: "Can you also will that which you will to will?" Thus we would be pushed back indefinitely, since we would think that a volition depended on a previous, deeper lying volition. In vain would we try to arrive in this way finally at a volition which we must think of and accept as dependent on nothing else. But if we were willing to accept such a volition, we could as well accept the first as the one we happened to make the last. Consequently, the question would be reduced to a simple: "Can you will?" But whether a mere affirmation of this question decides the problem of the freedom of the will, is what we wanted to know. So the problem remains unresolved.

We can see then that it is impossible to establish a direct connection between the concept of freedom—in its original, empirical meaning derived from action—and the concept of willing. In order nevertheless to be in a position to apply the concept of freedom to the will, one had to modify this concept by interpreting it more abstractly. This was accomplished by making the concept of freedom signify in general only the absence of any *necessity*. Thus interpreted, the concept retained its negative character, which I attributed to it from the very beginning. Accordingly, one must first investigate the concept of necessity, for this is the positive concept which gives meaning to the negative one.

So let us ask: What does one mean by "necessary"? The usual explanation: "necessary is that whose opposite is impossible, or which cannot be otherwise," is a mere word-definition, or paraphrase of the concept, which does not increase our understanding. As a real definition I propose the following: Something is necessary which follows from a given sufficient ground. This sentence, like any correct definition, can also be reversed. Depending on whether the ground in question is logical, or mathematical, or physical (i.e., called a cause), the necessity will be logical (e.g., of a conclusion, given the premises), or mathematical (e.g., equality of the sides of a triangle, given the equality of the angles), or physical, real (e.g., the occurrence of the effect, as soon as the cause is present). In all these cases, with equal strictness, the necessity is attached to the consequent when the ground is given. Only in so far as we comprehend something as the consequent of a given ground do we recognize it to be necessary. Conversely, as soon as we recognize something to be a consequent of a sufficient ground, we see that it is necessary. This is so because all grounds are compelling. This real definition is so adequate and exhaustive that the concept of necessity and the concept of consequent of a given sufficient ground are exchangeable concepts. In all cases, the one can be put in the place of the other.[3]

According to this, the absence of necessity would be identical with the absence of a determining sufficient ground. Still, we think of the *accidental* as the opposite of the *necessary*. But there is no conflict between these two views; each acciden-

[3] There is a discussion of the concept of necessity in my essay on the *Principle of Sufficient Reason*, Second Ed., § 49.

tal occurrence is only relatively so. For in the world of reality, where alone accidents can be encountered, every event is necessary in relation to its cause, while in relation to all other events which are contemporaneous and spatially contiguous with it, the event is accidental. But since the mark of freedom is absence of necessity, that which is free would have to be absolutely independent of any cause and would therefore have to be defined as absolutely accidental. This is a most problematic notion, and I don't guarantee that it is even conceivable. Nevertheless, it coincides in a singular fashion with the concept of freedom.

At any rate, that which is free remains that which is in no respect necessary, that is, not dependent on any ground. If this concept were applied to the will of man, this would mean that an individual will in its manifestations (volitions) would not be determined by causes or by sufficient grounds at all. Besides, since the consequent of a given ground (of whatever kind this may be) is always necessary, a man's acts would not be free but necessary. On this rests Kant's definition, according to which freedom is the capacity to initiate of oneself a series of changes. For in its true signification the expression "of oneself" means "without antecedent cause." This, however, is the same as "without necessity." So that, even though that definition gives to the concept of freedom the appearance of being positive, upon close scrutiny its negative nature emerges again.

A free will then would be the will which is not determined by grounds—and since everything that determines another must be a ground, in real things a real ground, that is, a cause—a free will would not be determined by anything at all. The particular manifestations of this will (volitions) would then proceed absolutely and quite originally from the will itself, without being brought about necessarily by antecedent conditions, and hence also without being determined by anything according to a rule. When we try to deal with this concept, clear thinking abandons us because, while the positing of a ground, in all of its meanings, is the essential form of our entire cognitive faculty, we are here asked to refrain from positing a ground. Still, there is no lack of a technical term also for this concept: this is *liberum arbitrium indifferentiae.* This is, by the way, the only clearly defined, firm, and positive concept of that which is called freedom of the will. One cannot therefore get away from it without involving oneself in vacillating, hazy explanations, behind which hides hesitant indecision, as when one talks about grounds which do not necessarily bring about their consequents. Every consequent of a ground is necessary, and every necessity is the consequent of a ground. The positing of such a free will of indifference has an immediate consequence which characterizes this concept and must therefore be regarded as its peculiar feature. This is that for a human individual equipped with such a feature, under given external conditions which are thoroughly determined in every particular, two diametrically opposed actions are equally possible.

2) What is the self-consciousness?

Answer: The consciousness of one's own self, in contrast to the consciousness of *other* things; this latter being the cognitive faculty. To be sure, even before those other things appear in it, this faculty contains certain forms of the manner of this occurrence. These forms are accordingly conditions of the possibility of objective being of things, that is, of their existing for us as objects. They are, as is well known, time, space, and causality. Now, although we find these forms of understanding in ourselves, their only purpose is that we can become conscious of other things as such, and be put in a definite relation to them. Therefore, even though these forms are contained in us, we must look upon them not as belonging to the self-consciousness, but rather as making possible the consciousness of other things, that is, our objective knowledge.

Further, the ambiguity of the word *conscientia,* used in the question, will not mislead me into loading the self-consciousness with the moral impulses known under the name of conscience or of practical reason together with its categorical imperatives affirmed by Kant. This should not be done, first, because these impulses appear only as a result of experience and reflection, hence as a result of the consciousness of other things, and second, because the borderline between that in them which belongs originally and properly to human nature and that which is added by moral and religious education, is not yet sharply and indisputably drawn. Moreover, it cannot possibly be the intention of the Royal Society to have the question transplanted onto the ground of morality by including conscience in the self-consciousness, and to see a restatement of Kant's moral proof—or rather postulate—of freedom from the a priori known moral laws, in virtue of the dictum, "you can because you ought."

From what has been said, it is evident that by far the greatest part of our entire consciousness in general is not our self-consciousness, but the consciousness of other things, or the cognitive faculty. The latter is directed outward with all its powers and is the scene (indeed, from a deeper point of investigation, the condition) of the real external world. At first our cognitive faculty grasps this world perceptively, but that which is thus obtained is forthwith worked over, as it were in a ruminating fashion, into concepts. Endless combinations of concepts, brought about with the help of words, constitute thinking. Only after we subtract this, by far the greatest part of our entire consciousness, do we get the self-consciousness. We already see that the content of the latter cannot be great. Hence, if the data required for the proof of the freedom of the will should really lie in the self-consciousness, we may hope that they will not escape us. An *inner sense* has also been set up as an organ of the self-consciousness.[4] But this must be taken in a metaphorical rather than in a real sense, because the self-consciousness is immediate. Be that as it may, our next question is: What does the self-conscious-

[4] It is found already in Cicero as *tactus interior: Acad. quaest.,* IV, 7. More explicitly in Augustine, *De lib. arb.,* II, 3 *sqq.* Then in Descartes, *Princ. phil.,* IV, 190; and quite developed in Locke.

ness contain? or How does man become directly conscious of his own self?

Answer: altogether as one who wills. In observing his own self-consciousness everyone will soon be aware that its object is always his own volitions. By this one must understand, to be sure, not only the deliberate acts of will which are immediately put into effect and the formal decisions together with the actions which follow from them. Whoever is capable of somehow discerning the essential element, even when it is disguised under various modifications of degree and kind, will not hesitate to include among the manifestations of will also all desiring, striving, wishing, demanding, longing, hoping, loving, rejoicing, jubilation, and the like, no less than not willing or resisting, all abhorring, fleeing, fearing, being angry, hating, mourning, suffering pains—in short, all emotions and passions. For these emotions and passions are weaker or stronger, violent and stormy or else quiet impulsions of one's own will, which is either restrained or unleashed, satisfied or unsatisfied. In their many variations they relate to the successful or frustrated attainment of that which is willed, to the endurance or the overcoming of that which is abhorred. Consequently, they are explicit affections of the same will which is active in decisions and actions.[5] To this context belongs even that which goes under the name of feelings of pleasure and of displeasure. Of course, these are present in a great variety of degrees and kinds, but still they can always be traced to the affections of desiring or abhorring, that is, to the will itself becoming aware of itself as satisfied or unsatisfied,

[5] It is well worth noting that the church father Augustine recognized this fully, while many modern thinkers, with their alleged "feeling faculty," do not see it. Namely in *De Civit. Dei,* Lib. XIV, c. 6, he speaks of affections of the soul, which in the previous book he brought under the four categories of desire, fear, joy, sadness, and says, "For the will is in them all; yea, none of them is anything else than will. For what are desire and joy but a volition of consent to the things we wish? And what are fear and sadness but a volition of aversion from the things we do not wish?" [Cf. Augustine's *The City of God* transl. M. Dods (Edinburgh: 1872), p. 9.—Tr.]

restrained or unleashed. Indeed, here should be included the bodily emotions, pleasant or painful, and all the innumerable others which lie between these two, since the nature of these emotions consists in this: they enter directly into the self-consciousness as either something which is in accordance with the will or something which opposes it. Even of his own body one is directly conscious, strictly speaking, only as the externally active organ of the will and as the seat of receptivity for pleasant or unpleasant sensations. But these sensations themselves, as just said, refer back to the quite immediate affections of the will which either conform or are opposed to it. For that matter, we may or may not include here these mere feelings of pleasure or displeasure, but in any case we find that all those movements of the will—that alternate wanting and not wanting, which in its constant ebb and flow constitutes the only object of the self-consciousness, or, if one prefers, of the inner sense—stand in a universal and generally acknowledged relation to that which is perceived and known in the external world. But that, as we have seen, lies no longer in the realm of the immediate self-consciousness. Consequently, we have arrived at the borderline of the self-consciousness as soon as we touched the external world, where the self-consciousness touches on the realm of the consciousness of other things. But the objects apprehended in the world are the material and the occasion for all those movements and acts of will. One will not interpret this as begging the question, for no one can deny that our willing always has external things for its object. It is directed toward them, it revolves around them, and is at least motivated by them. To think otherwise is to see the will as completely cut off from the external world and locked up in the dark recesses of the self-consciousness. The only issue which is still problematical for us here is the necessity with which the things located in the external world determine volition.

Thus we find that the self-consciousness is intensely, really even exclusively, occupied with willing. But does this sole content of the self-consciousness furnish data from which could be inferred the *freedom* of that very willing in the only distinct and definite sense of the word set forth above? To establish this is our end in view, and we shall now steer straight toward it. So far we have approached it only indirectly, and yet we have come noticeably closer to it.

THE WILL AND THE SELF-CONSCIOUSNESS

When a man wills, he wills something; his will is always directed to an object and can be thought of only in relation to an object. What does it mean then to will something? It means the following: the volition, which initially is itself only an object of the self-consciousness, comes into being as a result of something which belongs to the consciousness of other things and hence is an object of the cognitive faculty. In this relation the object is called a *motive* and constitutes at the same time the content of the volition. The volition is directed toward this object, i.e., it intends to change the object in some way and so reacts to it: its entire nature consists in this *reaction*. From this it is already evident that without such an object a volition could not take place, because then it would lack both reason and substance. But the question is whether, given the existence of this object for cognition, the volition *must* take place, or whether it may fail to occur, so that either no volition at all, or a quite different one, even the opposite, could arise. In other words, could that reaction fail to take place, could it be different or even contrary, under the very same set of circumstances? This means in brief: does the entrance of a motive into the consciousness necessarily bring about the volition, or does the will retain complete freedom either to will or not to will?

Here therefore the concept of freedom is taken as a mere negation of necessity, that is, in that abstract sense which was discussed above and shown to be solely applicable in this context; and so our problem is defined. But we have to seek the data for the solution of this problem in the immediate self-consciousness, and with this end in view we shall examine its evidence carefully. Still, we shall not reach a summary

14

decision by cutting the knot asunder in the manner of Descartes, who simply maintained: "We are so conscious of the freedom and indeterminacy which exist in us, that there is nothing that we comprehend more clearly and perfectly." [1] The invalidity of this thesis was already censured by Leibniz.[2] But on this point Leibniz himself was only a feeble straw in the wind; after making the most self-contradictory assertions, he came to the conclusion that the will is, to be sure, inclined but is not necessitated by motives. He says, "All actions are determined and never indifferent because there is always a ground which, even though it does not necessitate, inclines us to act thus and not otherwise." [3] This gives me an occasion to observe that such a middle way between the above-described alternatives is not tenable and that one cannot say, with a certain favorite half-heartedness, that the motives determine the will only to some extent, that it experiences their influence, but only to a certain degree, and can then free itself of that influence. For as soon as we have granted causality to a given force, that is, have recognized it as effective, then when this force encounters resistance, the only requirement for this force to fulfill its task is to be increased in proportion to the exerted resistance. He who cannot be bribed by 10 ducats but wavers, will succumb to 100 ducats, and so on.

So let us now turn with our problem to the immediate self-consciousness, in the sense in which it was established above. What does this self-consciousness reveal regarding that abstract question, namely, the question whether the concept of necessity is or is not applicable to the occurrence of volition when a motive is given, i.e., presented to the intellect? Or, what does it say about the possibility or impossibility of a volition's failing to occur in such a case? We would find our-

1 [René Descartes, *The Principles of Philosophy* (Cambridge: 1911), p. 235, trans. Haldane and Ross.—Tr.]

2 [Leibniz, *Theodicy*, I, § 50, and III, § 292.—Tr.]

3 [Leibniz, *On Freedom*. Schopenhauer refers to *De libertate*, *Opera* edition Erdmann, p. 669.]

selves much deluded if we expected from this self-consciousness fundamental and penetrating revelations about causality in general and motivation in particular, as well as about any necessity which they may carry with them. This is so because the self-consciousness, as it is indwelling in all men, is too simple and limited a thing to say anything about these matters. It is rather the case that these concepts are taken from pure understanding which is directed outward and can first of all be made to speak before the forum of the reflective reason. On the other hand, that natural, simple, and indeed innocent self-consciousness cannot even understand the question, to say nothing of not being able to answer it.

As everyone may find out by introspection, that which the self-consciousness says about volitions, when freed of all foreign and inessential elements and reduced to its naked content, can be expressed by something like this: "I can will, and if I will an action, the movable members of my body will immediately perform it as soon as I will it, quite without fail." This means, in brief: "I can do what I will." Farther than this the assertion of the immediate self-consciousness does not go, no matter how one may try to turn it about and in what way one asks the question. What it asserts then always refers to the ability to act in accordance with the will. But this is the empirical, original, and popular concept of freedom which we set up at the very beginning, and according to which "free" means "in accordance with the will." The self-consciousness will absolutely affirm this freedom. But that is not the freedom we are asking about. The self-consciousness affirms the freedom of action—when the willing is presupposed. But what is being inquired into is precisely the freedom of *willing*.

We are searching for the relationship of the willing itself to the motive, and about this the assertion "I can do what I will" says nothing. The self-consciousness does indeed affirm the dependence of our behavior, that is, of our bodily actions, on our will. But this dependence is something quite different from an independence of external circumstances on the part of our volitions. Such an independence *would* constitute the freedom of the will, but the self-consciousness can assert nothing about it, because this independence lies outside of its sphere, as it concerns the causal relationship of the external world to our decisions (which is given to us as the consciousness of other things). The self-consciousness cannot judge of the relation of that which lies entirely outside its sphere to that which lies within it. For no cognitive faculty can establish a relationship one of whose terms is not given to it in any fashion. But obviously the objects of willing which determine a volition lie outside the boundary of the self-consciousness, namely in the consciousness of other things, while the volition itself is contained only in the self-consciousness. We, however, are inquiring into the causal relation of those other things to the self-consciousness.

The business of the self-consciousness is only the volition, together with its absolute power over the parts of the body, which power is actually meant in the expression "what I will." Moreover, only the *use* of this power, i.e., the act, makes of it a volition, even for the self-consciousness. For as long as it is in the process of becoming it is called a wish; when completed, a resolve, but that it *is* a resolve is proved to the self-consciousness itself only by the act; up to this latter the volition is alterable. And here we are already at the very source of that appearance, to be sure an undeniable one, on the strength of which the layman (that is, the philosophically untrained person) thinks that in any given case two contrary volitions are possible for him. While saying this he presumes upon his self-consciousness, which, he thinks, has asserted this. Actually, he mistakes wishing for willing.

He can *wish* two opposing actions,[4] but *will* only one of them. Only the act reveals to his self-consciousness which of the two he wills. But as to the law-like necessity, by virtue of which the one of the two contrary wishes but not the other becomes volition and act, the self-consciousness can contain nothing, because it learns of the effect entirely a posteriori and does not know it a priori. Alternately and repeatedly,

[4] See *Parerga*, Vol. 2, § 327 of the first (§ 339 of the second) edition.

contrary wishes together with their motives rise and fall before the self-consciousness, and about each of them it states that it will become an act if it becomes a volition. For this latter, purely subjective possibility does indeed exist for each of them and is precisely the "I can do what I will." However, this subjective possibility is entirely hypothetical; it only means: "if I will this, I can do it." But the determination required for the willing is not contained in it, because the self-consciousness contains only the willing but not the grounds which determine the willing; the latter are found in the consciousness of other things, that is, in the cognitive faculty. On the contrary, it is the *objective* possibility that is decisive, but this lies outside the self-consciousness in the world of objects, to which belong both the motive and the man as an object. Therefore, this objective possibility is foreign to the self-consciousness and belongs to the consciousness of other things. That subjective possibility is of the same kind as that which enables a stone to give off sparks, but is nevertheless dependent on steel in which the objective possibility inheres. I shall return to this point from another direction in the following section. There we shall consider the will no longer from the inside, as we are doing here, but from the outside, and thus shall examine the objective possibility of volition. After thus being illuminated from two different sides, our problem will then attain its full clarity and will also be elucidated by means of examples.

Thus the feeling "I can do what I will," contained in the self-consciousness, always accompanies us, but signifies only that the decisions or definite acts of our will, even though they originate in the dark recesses of our inwardness, will always enter the perceptible world at once, since our body, like everything else, belongs to this world. This consciousness forms a bridge between the inner and the outer worlds which otherwise remained separated by a bottomless abyss. Without this bridge the outer world would contain mere perceptions as objects independent of us in every sense, and the inner world nothing but ineffective and merely felt volitions.

If we were to ask an unsophisticated person to describe that immediate consciousness which is so often regarded as that of an alleged freedom of the will, we would get something like the following answer: "I can do what I will: if I will to go to the left, I go to the left; if I will to go to the right, I go to the right. This depends entirely on my will; therefore, I am free." Of course this assertion is entirely true and correct, only the will is already presupposed in it, for it assumes that the will has already decided. Consequently, nothing can be established about its own freedom in this manner. The assertion does not at all speak about the dependence or independence of the *occurrence* of the act of volition itself, but only about the *effects* of this act as soon as it occurs, or, to be more precise, about its unfailing manifestation as bodily action. It is, however, nothing but the consciousness underlying this assertion that leads the layman, that is, the philosophically untrained person—who nevertheless in other areas can be very learned—to regard the freedom of the will as so immediately certain that he expresses it as indubitable truth and cannot really believe that philosophers seriously doubt it. Such a man believes in his heart that all this loose talk is a mere sparring exercise in academic dialectic and is at bottom a joke.

The certainty which is given to man through that consciousness and is indeed important is always very much at hand. Moreover, as primarily and essentially a practical, not a theoretical being, man is much more distinctly conscious of the active aspect of his volitions, that is, of their effectiveness, than of the passive aspect, that is, of their dependence. It is precisely for these reasons that it is difficult to make clear to a philosophically untrained person the real meaning of our problem and to make him understand that the question now is not about the *effects* but about the *grounds* of each act of willing. We grant that his *acting* depends entirely on his willing, but now we want to know on what his willing itself depends. Does it depend on nothing at all or on something? Of course, we say, he can do one thing when he wills it, and he can just as well do another thing when he wills it, but he should now consider whether he is able to will the one thing quite as well as the other. If, with this intention in mind, we ask a man a question like the following: "When two contrary wishes arise in you, can you really comply with the one just as well as with the other? For example, when you are to choose between two mutually exclusive objects of possession, can you prefer one as well as the other?" He will say: "Perhaps the choice will be difficult for me, but it will always depend completely on me whether I will choose one or the other and on no other power. I have complete freedom as to which of the two I shall will to choose, and in this I shall always follow my will alone." Now if one says: "But your willing itself, on what does *it* depend?", the man will fall back on the self-consciousness: "On nothing else but myself. I can will what I will: what I will, that I will." And he says this without intending it to be a tautology, or without even leaning in his innermost consciousness on the law of identity, by virtue of which alone this is true. But rather, being very hard put to it, he talks about a willing of his willing, which is the same as if he talked about the self of his self. One has pushed him back to the very heart of his self-consciousness, where he encounters his self and his will as indistinguishable, but where nothing remains to pass judgment on both of them.

The question is whether in that choice—assuming as given his person and the objects of his choice—his own willing of one thing and not the other could possibly have been somehow different from what it actually was, or whether, by virtue of the given data, his willing was as necessarily determined as is the fact that in a triangle the largest side lies opposite the largest angle. This question is so far removed from the natural self-consciousness that the latter even fails to comprehend the question, to say nothing of its containing the answer to it ready made, or even only as an undeveloped germ, which it would merely need to hand out naively. As already indicated, then, the ingenuous but philosophically untrained man will still try to escape the perplexity which the question, when really understood, must bring about, by hiding behind that immediate certainty "what I will, I can do, and I will what I will," as has been said above. This he will try again and again, countless times, so that it will be difficult to confront him with the real question, from which he all the time tries to escape. And one should not blame him for it, because the question is indeed most delicate. It penetrates searchingly into the very innermost being of man: it wants to know whether he also, like everything else in the world, is a being determined once for all by his own constitution which, like everything else in nature, has its definite, persisting properties, from which his reactions issue necessarily upon the occurrence of external stimuli. It wants to know whether, accordingly, these properties have an unalterable character in this respect, which leaves any possible modification in them fully at the mercy of determination by external stimuli, or whether man alone constitutes an exception to the whole of nature.

Should one finally succeed in confronting him with this delicate question and should one make clear to him that what is being searched for is the origin of his volitions themselves— whether they are subject to some rule or whether their emergence is completely lawless—one will discover that on this score no information is contained in the immediate self-consciousness. Our ingenuous man himself stops trying here and reveals his perplexity by sinking into deep meditation and by attempting all sorts of explanations. One time he tries to ground them in the experiences he has with himself or with others, another time in general rules of understanding. But in all this, the uncertainty and the vacillation of his explanations show clearly enough that his immediate self-consciousness provides no information on the correctly understood question, while in respect to the question erroneously interpreted it was quite ready to give an answer. In the final analysis this is due to the fact that man's will is his authentic self, the true core of his being; hence it constitutes the ground of his consciousness as something which is simply given and present and beyond which he cannot go. For he himself is as he wills, and wills as he is. Therefore to ask him whether he could also will differently than he does is to ask whether he could also be other than himself; and that he does not know. For this very reason the philosopher, who differs from such a man only by virtue of his training, if he is to arrive at clarity in this difficult matter, must turn to his understanding, which provides knowledge a priori, to his reason, which reflects on such knowledge, and, as the final and the only competent court of appeal, to experience, which presents to him his acts and the acts of others, so that such apperceptions of the understanding can be interpreted and checked. The decision of this tribunal is, to be sure, not as easy, as immediate and simple as that of the self-consciousness, and yet in compensation it will be to the point and sufficient. It is the head that has posed the question, and the head must answer it.

Anyway, we should not be surprised that the immediate self-consciousness is not in possession of an answer to that abstruse, speculative, difficult, and delicate question. For the self-consciousness is a very limited part of our entire consciousness. While inwardly obscure, our consciousness is oriented, with all its objective cognitive powers, entirely outward. All of its completely assured, that is, a priori certain, cognitions concern only the external world, and in that area it can judge with assurance, in accordance with certain general laws which are rooted in itself, what in that outside world is possible, impossible, and necessary; and in this way it brings into being a priori pure mathematics, pure logic, indeed pure basic natural science. Accordingly, the application of its a priori conscious forms to the data given in sensation provides the perceptible, real external world and therewith experience; further, when to this external world logic is applied and the faculty of thought which underlies logic, we get concepts or the world of ideas, and these again yield the sciences, their achievements, etc. Thus it is there, on the *outside;* great clarity and illumination spread themselves before the gaze of the consciousness. But on the inside it is dark like a thoroughly blackened telescope. No a priori proposition illuminates the night of its interior; these lighthouses shine only toward the outside. As was discussed above, to the so-called inner sense nothing is present except our own will, and properly all so-called inner feelings must be traced back to its movements. But as shown above, everything that produces this inner perception of the will reverts to willing and not willing, accompanied by the commended certainty "what I will, that I can do," which really means: "I see every act of my will present itself to me immediately (in a way which is quite inexplicable to me) as an action of my body," and which, strictly speaking, is a proposition of experience for the knowing subject. More than that nothing can be found here. Therefore, the tribunal to which we turned is incompetent to deal with the question raised. Indeed, in its true sense, the question cannot even be brought before it, because this tribunal does not understand it.

The answer which we received from the self-consciousness in response to our question I shall now restate in a shorter and easier wording. Everyone's self-consciousness asserts very clearly that he can do what he wills. But since we can conceive of him as willing quite opposite actions, it follows that if he so wills he can also *do* the opposite. Now the untutored understanding confuses this with the proposition that he, in a given case, can also *will* the opposite, and calls this the freedom of the will. But that in any given case he can will the opposite is absolutely not contained in the above proposition, but only this, namely, that of two contrary actions he can perform one action, if he wills it, or he can likewise perform the other one, if he wills that. But whether in a given case he can *will* the one as well as the other remains undetermined and calls for a deeper investigation than the one which mere self-consciousness could decide. The shortest, even though scholastic, formula for this result would be: the assertion of the self-consciousness concerns the will only *a parte post;* the question of freedom, on the other hand, *a parte ante.*

Hence, that undeniable assertion of the self-consciousness, "I can do what I will," contains and decides nothing at all about the freedom of the will. This freedom would consist in this, that the actual volition in each particular case and for a given particular character would not be determined necessarily by the external circumstances in which this man found himself, but could turn out now this way and now another way. But on this point the self-consciousness remains completely silent; for the matter lies entirely outside its realm, since it rests on the causal relation between the external world and the man. Ask a man who is of sound mind but who has no philosophical training in what the freedom of the will consists, which he so confidently maintained on the basis of the assertion of his self-consciousness, and he will answer: "It consists in this: I can do what I will provided I am not hindered physically." Hence it is always the relation of his acting to his willing that he speaks of. But this, as has been shown in the first section, is still merely *physical* freedom. If one asks him further whether in a given case he can will the one thing as well as he can its opposite, he will in his first zeal, to be sure, affirm this. But as soon as he starts to grasp the meaning of the question he will begin to have doubts, finally sink into uncertainty and confusion, and again prefer to take refuge behind his thesis "I can do what I will." There he will fortify himself against all grounds and all reasoning. But the corrected answer to his thesis, as I hope to free from all doubt in the next section, would be as follows: "You can do what you will, but in any given moment of your life you can *will* only one definite thing and absolutely nothing other than that one thing."

The question of the Royal Society, really, has now been answered by the discussion contained in this section, and answered negatively. To be sure, this has been done only in the main, and in what is to follow the actual state of affairs with regard to the self-consciousness will be presented more fully. But even this negative answer of ours can be still further checked up in one instance. Namely, we might address the question to that authority to which in the foregoing we were directed as the only competent authority, i.e., to the pure understanding, to reason as it reflects on the data of the latter, and to experience which accompanies both. The verdict of this authority would be to the effect that a *liberum arbitrium* does not exist at all, but that the actions of men, like everything else in nature, take place in any given case as an effect which follows necessarily. This authority would give us in addition the assurance that the data from which the alleged *liberum arbitrium* could be proved *cannot even be located* in the immediate self-consciousness. In this way, by means of the argument *a non posse ad non esse,* which is the only possible way of establishing negative truths a priori, our decision could get a rational foundation besides the already presented empirical one, and hence would be doubly secured. For a decided contradiction between the immediate statements of the self-consciousness and the conclusions from the principles of human understanding, together with their application to experience, cannot be accepted as possible; our self-consciousness cannot be so mendacious. In this connection it should be noted that the ostensible antinomy which Kant put forward on this subject does not arise even for him from the fact that the thesis and antithesis come from different cognitive sources: one from the statements of the self-consciousness, the other from reason and experience; but both thesis and antithesis rationalize too subtly from allegedly objective grounds. But while the thesis rests on nothing more than stagnant reason, that is, on the need to find some stopping point in the regress, the antithesis really has all the objective grounds on its side.

While the indirect investigation which is to be now undertaken deals with the field of cognitive faculty and with the external world spread out before it, it will at the same time throw much light on the direct investigation so far carried out and thus will serve as its completion. It will disclose the natural delusions arising from the false interpretations of that so utterly simple statement of the self-consciousness when the latter conflicts with the awareness of other things, that is, with the cognitive faculty which is rooted along with the self-consciousness in one and the same subject. Indeed, the true meaning and content of that "I will" which accompanies all our actions and the nature of the consciousness of originality and arbitrariness by virtue of which they are *our* actions will dawn upon us only at the end of this indirect study. Whereby the direct investigation so far carried out will finally reach its completion.

THE WILL AND THE CONSCIOUSNESS OF OTHER THINGS

Turning now to the cognitive faculty with our problem, we know beforehand that, since this faculty is essentially directed outward, it cannot perceive the will immediately as the self-consciousness does. But we found the self-consciousness incompetent to deal with our problem. The cognitive faculty, on the other hand, must consider only the *beings* which are equipped with will. These beings stand before the cognitive faculty as objective and external phenomena, that is, as objects of experience; as such they are to be investigated and judged, partly in accordance with universal, a priori certain rules, which are valid for all possible experience, and partly in accordance with the facts which the ready-made and actually present experience provides.

Hence we are no longer dealing here with the will itself as accessible only to the inner sense, but with those beings which will or are moved by the will, and which are the objects of the external senses. Even though in this procedure we suffer from the disadvantage of having to consider the actual object of our investigation only mediately and from a greater distance, this is outweighed by the advantage that we can now make use of a much more perfect instrument in our investigation than the dark, dull, one-sided, immediate self-consciousness, or the so-called inner sense. We can now use the understanding, equipped for objective apprehension with all external senses and all powers.

We find the most universal and fundamentally essential form of this understanding to be the law of causality. For only by the mediation of this law is the perception of the real external world brought about, whereby immediately and quite directly we apprehend as "effects" the affections and changes felt in our sense-organs and (without guidance, teaching, and experience) at once make a transition from them to their "causes." Precisely through this process of understanding, these "causes" now present themselves to us as objects in space.[1] From this it is incontestably evident that we are a priori aware of the law of causality, which is consequently *necessary* for the possibility of any experience.

For this we need not resort to the indirect, difficult, indeed insufficient proof which Kant supplied for this important truth. The law of causality is established a priori as the general rule to which all objects of the external world are subject without exception. This lack of exceptions is owing to its a priori character. The law refers essentially and exclusively to *changes* and means that wherever and whenever in the objective, real, material world *anything* changes to a lesser or greater extent, something else must necessarily have changed just before it, and that "something else" before that, and prior to that another one, and so on to infinity, without our ever seeing any starting point of this regressive series of changes which fill time as matter fills space. Such a starting point could not be thought possible, to say nothing of its being presupposed. For the question, which unremittingly renews itself, "What brought this change about?" never grants the understanding a final resting point, no matter how it may weary. For this reason a first cause is just as unthinkable as a beginning of time or a limit of space. The law of causality means no less definitely that when the earlier change—the cause—has occurred, then the later one which it brought about—the effect—must occur quite inevitably and therefore takes place necessarily.

Through this character of necessity the law of causality qualifies as a manifestation of the principle of sufficient reason, which is the most universal form of our entire cognitive faculty. As it appears in the real world as causality, so in the

[1] A detailed discussion of this doctrine can be found in the treatise on the Principle of Sufficient Reason, § 21.

world of ideas as the logical law of cognitive ground. Even in the empty but a priori intuited space this principle appears as the law of the strictly necessary mutual interdependence in position of all parts of it; to prove this necessary dependence specifically and in detail is the sole subject matter of geometry. Just for this reason, as my initial discussion showed, to be necessary and to be the consequent of a given ground are interchangeable concepts.

Hence all changes taking place in the objects contained in the real external world are subject to the law of causality, and therefore, wherever and whenever they occur, they always occur necessarily and inevitably. To this there can be no exception, since the rule exists a priori for all the possibilities of experience. But as to its application to any given case one must only ask whether it concerns a change of a real object given in external experience. If it does, then its changes are subject to the application of the law of causality; that is, they must be brought about by a cause, but just for that reason *necessarily*.

Let us now use our general rule, which is a priori certain and therefore valid for all possible experience without exception, to look at this experience somewhat more closely. If we consider the real objects which are given in it and to whose changes our rule refers, we soon observe in these objects some far-reaching basic differences, according to which they have long since been classified. These objects are in part inorganic, that is, lifeless, in part organic, that is, living. The latter can be in turn divided into plants and animals. Furthermore, although all animals are similar to one another in essentials and correspond to one concept, still they constitute a most varied and finely differentiated hierarchy of perfection, beginning with those which still are closely related to plants and only with difficulty distinguishable from them, and ending with the most highly perfected beings which correspond most completely to the concept of animal. At the summit of this hierarchy we see the human being—ourselves.

If we do not let ourselves be misled by that diversity, but

consider all these beings as objective, real subjects of experience, and proceed to apply to the changes taking place in them our a priori established law of causality which makes all experience possible, we shall find that, even though experience always agrees with the a priori certain law, yet to the above enumerated great differences in the nature of all these objects of experience there also corresponds an appropriate modification of the way in which causality applies its jurisdiction to them. More precisely: corresponding to the three-fold difference between inorganic bodies, plants, and animals, the causality which guides all their changes appears likewise in three forms, namely as *cause* in the narrowest sense of the word, or as *stimulus,* or as *motivation.* Through this modification the a priori validity of causality and consequently the necessity of the effect which it imposes are not in the least impaired.

"Cause" in the narrowest sense of the word is that whereby all mechanical, physical, and chemical changes in the objects of experience take place. It is always characterized by two features. First, to it applies Newton's third law, "action and reaction are equal to one another," that is, the antecedent state, called cause, experiences the same change as the following state, called effect. Second, according to Newton's second law, the degree of the effect always corresponds exactly to the degree of the cause. The strengthening of one therefore brings about an equal strengthening of the other, so that, when once the type of effect is known, the degree of the effect can be immediately known, measured and calculated from the degree of the intensity of the cause, and vice versa.

However, in the empirical application of this second feature one must not confuse the real effect with its visible appearance. For instance, one should not expect that when a body is compressed its volume will keep decreasing in proportion to the increase of the compressing force. For the space into which the body is forced always decreases and, consequently, its resistance increases. So that even though the actual effect in this case, namely the condensation, actually grows in proportion to the cause according to Mariotte's law, this fact cannot be read off from that visible appearance. Further, when water is heated, up to a certain point the heat will bring about an increase in temperature, but beyond this point it will cause only a quick evaporation. But here again the same relationship between the degree of the cause and that of the effect holds—and so in many other cases.

Such are then the causes in the narrowest sense which effect changes in all lifeless, that is, inorganic bodies. The knowledge and the presupposition of causes of this type guides the investigation of all the changes which are the subject matter of mechanics, hydro-dynamics, physics, and chemistry. Being exclusively determined by causes of this type is therefore the real and essential characteristic of an inorganic or lifeless body.

The second type of cause is the *stimulus,* that is, a cause which, first, does not itself experience a reaction caused by its action, and second, does not at all exhibit uniformity between its intensity and the intensity of its effect. Consequently, here the degree of the effect cannot be measured and determined beforehand from the degree of the cause. Rather, a small increase of the stimulus can cause a very great increase of the effect, or, quite the opposite, it may do away altogether with the antecedently produced effect, indeed it may bring about a contrary one. For example, as is well known, the growth of plants can be extraordinarily speeded up by means of heat or by adding calcium to the soil, since these causes stimulate their life force. If, however, the stimulus goes a little beyond the proper degree, instead of enhancing and accelerating the life of the plant, it will kill it. In the same fashion, by means of wine or opium we can intensify and considerably heighten our mental powers, but as soon as the right measure of stimulus is exceeded, the effect will be exactly the opposite.

This type of causes, namely stimuli, is the one which determines all changes of organisms as such. All changes and developments of plants, and all merely organic and vegetative

changes or functions of animal bodies occur in response to
stimuli. This is the way in which light, heat, air, nourishment,
every chemical, every contact, fertilization, etc., act on them.
While the life of animals has besides this still another, quite
different, area, of which I shall soon speak, the entire life of
plants proceeds in response to stimuli. Assimilation, growth,
striving of the tree top toward the light, of the roots toward
better soil, fertilization, sprouting, etc.—all of these are
changes in response to stimuli. In some few species a peculiar
quick motion is added which likewise occurs only upon stimuli; however, they are called sensitive plants because of this.
As is well known, these are primarily *Mimosa pudica, Hedy-
sarum gyrans* and *Dionaea muscipula*. Determination by stimuli exclusively and without exception is the characteristic of
a plant. Accordingly, a plant is any body whose characteristic
changes and movements, appropriate to its nature, occur always and exclusively in response to stimuli.

The third type of activating causes is that which is characteristic of animals. This is *motivation,* that is, causality which
passes through cognition. In the hierarchy of natural organisms it enters at the point where, by virtue of having more
complicated and hence manifold needs, the creature could no
longer satisfy them in response to stimuli which must be
waited for; it also had to be in a position to choose, to grasp,
indeed to find the means of satisfaction. Therefore, in such
organisms, in place of the mere receptivity to stimuli and
the motion toward them, there enters a receptivity to motives,
in other words, an imaginative faculty, an intellect in countless stages of perfection. Materially this manifests itself as
nervous system and brain, and with these the consciousness
enters the stage. It is well known that plant life which as such
goes on only in response to stimuli serves as the basis of animal life. But all the movements which the animal performs as
animal and which depend precisely on what physiology calls
animal functions, take place as an effect of a cognized object,
hence in response to motives. Accordingly an animal is any
organism whose characteristic external movements and changes,

appropriate to its nature, are always the result of motives, that is, of certain ideas which are present to the already presupposed consciousness. Even though the capacity for ideas, and hence consciousness, may have infinite gradations in the series of animals, every animal has enough to become aware of a motive and to be moved by it. In this process, the inner moving power whose particular manifestation is brought about by the motive makes itself known to the now present self-consciousness as that which we designate by the word "will."

Now, for external observation, which is our standpoint here, it can never remain doubtful whether a given body moves in response to stimuli or to motives—so obviously different is the effectiveness of a stimulus from that of a motive. For a stimulus always acts by means of immediate contact, or even through absorption into itself, and wherever even this is not visible, as in the case of stimulation by air, light, or heat, it still reveals itself in the fact that the effect has an unmistakable relation to the duration and intensity of the stimulus, even though this relation does not stay the same for all degrees of stimulus. On the other hand, whenever a *motive* causes a movement, such distinctions disappear completely. For here the actual and the most proximate medium of influence is not the atmosphere, but cognition alone. The object which acts as motive needs absolutely nothing but to be perceived, cognized; and here it makes no difference at all how long, whether from near or far, and how distinctly it has entered the apperception. None of these distinctions in any way affect the degree of the effect: as soon as a motive is perceived it acts in exactly the same manner, provided that it can ever be a determining ground of the will which is to be excited in this case. For even the physical and chemical causes, and likewise the stimuli, have effects only in so far as the body to be affected is receptive to them. I just said, "of the will which is to be excited in this case," for, as already mentioned, that which actually gives to the motive the power to influence, in other words, the secret spring of the movement elicited by the motive, makes itself known to the organism inwardly and immediately as that which the word "will" designates.

In the case of bodies whose motions are mere responses to stimuli (plants), we call the life force that which persistently conditions from within. In the case of bodies which move merely in response to causes in the narrow sense, we call it natural force, or quality. In explanations this force is always presupposed as inexplicable, because within such beings there is no self-consciousness to which it would be immediately accessible. But whether, in the case of such un-perceiving or even lifeless beings this inner conditioning in them of their reaction to external causes—if one, ignoring appearances altogether, would wish to search for what Kant calls the thing-in-itself—whether this might be in its nature identical with that which in our selves we call the will, as a recent philosopher has actually tried to demonstrate—this I leave undecided, without necessarily intending to contest his view.[2]

On the other hand I must not leave unexplored the difference produced, in connection with motivation, by that which distinguishes the human consciousness from that of the animal. This feature, which the word "reason" really denotes, consists in the fact that man is not only able, like the animal, to grasp perceptually the external world, but also to abstract from it general concepts (*notiones universales*) to which he assigns words in order to fix them and keep them in his sensuous consciousness. With these words he then forms countless combinations. To be sure, like the concepts of which they consist, the combinations of words refer to the perceptually cognized world; nevertheless, they do really make up that which is called thinking and through which all the great advantages of mankind over all other beings are made possible, namely speech, reflectiveness, retrospection, concern for the future, intention, design, the planned, common action of many persons, the state, sciences, arts, etc. All this rests on the single ability to have non-perceptual, abstract, general ideas, called

[2] It is obvious that I am here speaking of myself. I could not speak in the first person because of the required incognito.

concepts (that is, essences of things), because each of these comprehends much detail within itself.

Animals, even the most clever ones, lack this ability; hence they have no ideas other than perceptual ones, and accordingly they know only that which is immediately present; they live only in the present. The motives by which their will is moved must, therefore, always be perceptual and actual. But the consequence of this is that they have extremely little choice. They can choose only among the things which spread themselves out perceptually before their limited field of vision and capacity to grasp, and so are present in time and space. That among them which is strongest as motive determines their will immediately, so that the causality of the motive is here very obvious. An apparent exception to this is made by training, which is fear operating through the medium of habit. A somewhat actual exception is instinct, insofar as by means of it in the total complex of its behavior the animal is set in motion not really by motives but through inner push and pull. However, in respect to particular actions and for every given moment, the proximate determination of this push and pull still proceeds from the motives, and thus reverts to the rule. A more detailed discussion of instinct would lead me too far from my subject; I deal with it in Chapter XXVII of the second volume of my main work.

On the other hand, by virtue of his capacity for non-perceptual ideas, by means of which he thinks and reflects, man has an infinitely larger field of vision, which includes the absent, the past, and the future. Because of this he can act from motives, and consequently exercise a choice, over a much greater range than the animal, which is limited to the narrow present. His action is not determined as a rule by that which lies before his sensuous perception and is present in space and time. Such determination proceeds rather from mere *thoughts* which he carries around everywhere in his head and which make him independent of the influence of the present. Whenever they fail to do that, one calls his actions irrational, and conversely, an action is praised as rational if it is performed strictly in accordance with well-considered thoughts and is therefore completely independent of the influence of the perceptual present. The very fact that man is activated by his own class of ideas (abstract concepts, thoughts), not possessed by the animal, is even externally visible. It impresses on all his actions, even the least significant ones, indeed on all his movements and steps, the character of the designed and intentional. Because of this, his activity is so visibly different from that of animals that one can positively see how his actions are guided, as it were, by fine, invisible threads (motives consisting of mere thoughts), whereas the actions of animals are pulled by rough, visible strings of what is perceptually present.

But the difference does not go further than that. The thought becomes a motive, as perception becomes a motive as soon as it can act on the particular will. All motives are causes, however, and all causality carries with it necessity. By means of his capacity to think, man can present to himself the motives whose influence on his will he feels in any order, alternately and repeatedly, in order to hold them up to his will. This is called deliberation. Man is capable of deliberation, and thanks to this capacity he has a far greater choice than is possible for the animal. Because of this he is, of course, relatively free. He is free of the immediate compulsion of the perceptually present objects which act as motives on his will. To this the animal is subject absolutely. Man, on the other hand, determines himself independently of the present objects, namely by thoughts, which are *his* motives.

At bottom, it is probably this relative freedom that educated yet not deeply thinking people understand by the freedom of the will, clearly putting man ahead of the animals. This freedom, however, is only relative, namely, in relation to that which is present in perception, and only comparative, namely, in comparison with the animal. By its means only the type of motivation is altered, while the necessity of the effect of motives is not in the least obliterated, or even diminished. An abstract motive, consisting in a mere thought, is an external cause determining the will just as much as is a perceptual one, consisting in an actual and present object. Consequently, it is a cause like any other, and even consists always, like the others, in something real and material, insofar as it always rests ultimately on some impression, received sometime and somewhere from the outside. It only has the advantage of a longer conducting wire, by which expression I want to convey the idea that it is not, like mere perceptual motives, bound to a certain proximity in space and time, but can act across the greatest distance, the longest time, and through a mediation of concepts and thoughts in a long concatenation. This is the consequence of the constitution and the eminent sensitivity of the organ which first experiences the action of the motive and takes it in, namely, of the human brain, or of reason. This, however, does not in the least abolish its causality, nor the necessity which causality involves. Only a very superficial view, therefore, can regard that relative and comparative freedom as an absolute one, a *liberum arbitrium indifferentiae.*

The ability to deliberate, which arises from this relative freedom, yields in reality nothing but the very frequently distressing conflict of motives, which is dominated by indecision and has the whole soul and consciousness of man as its battlefield. This conflict makes the motives try out repeatedly, against one another, their effectiveness on the will. This puts the will in the same situation as that of the body on which different forces act in opposite directions, until finally the decidedly strongest motive drives the others from the field and determines the will. This outcome is called resolve, and it takes place with complete necessity as the result of the struggle.

Let us survey once more the whole series of forms of causality which are clearly distinguished from one another. We have causes in the narrowest sense of the word, then stimuli, and finally motives, which in turn fall into perceptual and abstract. We shall observe, as we review in this respect the series of beings from the lower to the higher, that the cause and its effect recede more and more from one another, separate more

distinctly, and become more heterogeneous. The cause becomes less and less material and palpable, and hence seems to
contain less and less, while the effect seems to contain more
and more. When all this is taken together, the connection between cause and effect loses in immediate comprehensibility
and intelligibility. Least of all does this happen in the case of
mechanical causality, which for this reason can be compre-
hended best of all. This led in the last century to the mistaken
endeavor, which still persists in France but has recently also
come into fashion in Germany, to reduce every other causality
to the mechanical, and so to explain all physical and chemical
processes by mechanical causes, but the life process again by
the former.

The pushing body moves the one at rest and loses as much
motion as it communicates. Here we see the cause go over into
the effect, as it were; the two are quite homogeneous, exactly
commensurable, and palpable besides. And this is really the
case in respect to all purely mechanical effects. But one will
find that all this is less and less the case, and that on the contrary what we said above enters in, the higher we ascend. To
see this, consider at each level the relation between cause and
effect, as for instance between heat as cause and its various
effects: expansion, glowing, smelting, evaporating, burning,
thermo-electricity, etc.; or between evaporation as cause and
cooling-off, or crystallization, as effects; or between rubbing
glass as cause, and free electricity with its strange phenomena
as effect; or between the slow oxidation of metal plates as
cause, and galvanism, with all its electrical, chemical, and
magnetic phenomena, as effect. So cause and effect separate
more and more, become more heterogeneous, their connection
less comprehensible. The effect seems to contain more than
the cause could supply, since the latter shows itself as less and
less material and palpable.

All of this occurs even more clearly when we shift to the
organic bodies, where the causes are mere stimuli, partly external—such as those of light, heat, air, soil, and nourishment
—and partly internal—those of the saps and mutual influence

of parts; and where the effect of these stimuli is life, in its infinite complexity and countless varieties of type, in the multiple forms of plant and animal life.[3]

But has the relationship between cause and effect, because of the increasing heterogeneity, incommensurability, and incomprehensibility, lost any of the necessity required by this relationship? By no means—not in the least. As necessarily as the rolling ball sets in motion the one at rest, so must also the Leyden jar discharge when touched with the other hand, so must arsenic kill every living thing. So a seed which, preserved in dry condition, showed no change throughout thousands of years, as soon as it is put into proper soil and exposed to the action of air, light, heat, and moisture, must sprout, grow, and develop into a plant. The cause is more complicated, the effect more heterogeneous, but the necessity with which it takes place is not smaller by even a hair's breadth.

True, in the life of plants and in the vegetative life of animals the stimulus is in every respect most different from the organic function which it calls forth, and the two are distinctly separated. Still, they are not really parted, for a contact must be present between them, no matter how fine and invisible. Complete separation in animal life first occurs when actions are called forth by motives. In this process the cause, which up to this point was still materially related to the effect, is now completely disengaged from it and is of quite different nature: it is something initially immaterial, a mere idea. Hence in the case of a motive which originates the motion of an animal that heterogeneity between cause and effect, their separation from one another, their incommensurability, the immateriality of the cause and, consequently, its apparent lack of content as compared with the effect, has reached the highest degree.

The incomprehensibility of the relation between the two would become absolute if we knew this relation only from the

[3] A more detailed discussion of this separating of cause and effect can be found in *The Will in Nature*, section on Astronomy, p. 80ff. of the second (p. 87 of the third) edition.

outside, as we know all the other causal relationships. But as it is, a cognition of a wholly different sort, namely, an *inner* cognition, completes the external one. The process which takes place here as an effect after the occurrence of the cause is known to us intimately; we designate it by an *ad hoc* term: the will. But that here also the causal relationship has lost no necessity, as little as above in the case of the stimulus, we acknowledge as soon as we *recognize* it as a causal relationship and think of it by means of this form, so intrinsic to our reason.

Moreover, we find motivation to be fully analogous to the two above explained forms of causal relation, and see it only as the highest stage to which these forms rise in a quite gradual transition. On the lowest levels of animal life the motive is still closely related to stimulus: zoophytes and radiata in general, acephala among the molluscs, have only a feeble twilight of consciousness, just as much as is necessary to perceive their nourishment or prey and to snatch it when it offers itself, or at best to change their location to one more favorable. Hence the action of the motive on these low levels presents itself to us still quite as distinctly, immediately, decisively, and unambiguously as that of the stimulus. Small insects are drawn by the shining light into the very flame; flies alight trustfully on the head of a lizard that has just now consumed their fellows before their very eyes. Who will dream of freedom here? In the higher, more intelligent animals the action of motives becomes more and more indirect, that is, the motive separates itself more distinctly from the action to which it gives rise; so that one could even use this difference of the distance between the motive and the action as the standard of animal intelligence. In man this difference becomes immeasurable.

On the other hand, even in the cleverest animals the idea which becomes the motive of their action must still be perceptual. Even where a choice is already possible, it can take place only from among those things which are perceptually present. A dog stands hesitatingly between the call of his master and the sight of a she-dog; the stronger motive will determine his motion; but then it will take place as necessarily as a mechanical effect. Even as to mechanics we see that a body which is thrown out of equilibrium oscillates for a time alternately from one side to another until it is finally determined on which side lies its center of gravity—and then it falls to that side. As long as motivation is limited to perceptual ideas, its relation to stimulus and to cause in general becomes evident also from the fact that the motive, being an active cause, is something real and present; indeed, it must act physically on the senses, even though very indirectly by means of light, sound, and smell. Moreover, an observer can see the cause just as plainly as the effect. He sees the motive enter in and the action of the animal follow inevitably, as long as no other equally conspicuous motive or training counteracts it. It is impossible to doubt the connectedness of the two. Therefore it will not occur to anyone to ascribe to animals a *liberum arbitrium indifferentiae*, that is, actions which are not determined by a cause.

But where the consciousness is rational, that is, capable of a non-perceptual cognition, i.e., of concepts and thoughts, then the motives become quite independent of the present and the real surroundings, and are therefore hidden from the spectator. For then they are mere thoughts, which a man carries around in his head, whose origination is outside the head and often far removed from it: namely, now in the personal experience of past years, now in communications from others by spoken or written words, even from the most remote times. But still the origin of motives is in all cases real and objective, although, because of the frequently difficult combination of complicated external circumstances, among the motives there are also many mistakes, many handed-down illusions, and consequently many stupidities. In addition, very often a man hides the motives of his action from all others, sometimes even from himself, namely in those instances when he shrinks from knowing what really moves him to do this or that. Meanwhile, we see his actions take place and by means of conjectures seek to fathom the motives which we presuppose here just as firmly and confidently as we do the cause of every motion of lifeless bodies which we might have seen happen, fully convinced that without a cause neither the one nor the other is possible.

Conversely, in our own plans and undertakings we correspondingly take into account the effect of motives on men with an assurance which would fully equal the assurance with which we calculate the mechanical effects of mechanical devices, if we only knew with the same accuracy the individual characters of the people we are dealing with as we know the length and thickness of beams, the diameter of wheels, the weight of loads, etc. Everyone makes this assumption as long as he looks outward, has to do with others, and pursues practical ends; and the human mind is intended for this purpose. But if he tries to judge the matter theoretically and philosophically—for which purpose the human intelligence is not really intended—and makes himself the object of judgment, then he allows himself to be misled by the just described immaterial nature of abstract motives which consist of mere thoughts. Because such motives are not bound to any present and any specific surroundings, and because the obstacles to them in turn consist of mere thoughts as countermotives, this man is brought so far that he even doubts their existence or the necessity of their effects and thinks that whatever is done could just as well remain not done, that the will decides all by itself, without any cause, and that every one of his acts is the beginning of an incalculable series of changes it had initiated.

This error gains a special support from the false interpretation of the assertion of the self-consciousness, "I can do what I will," which was extensively examined in the first section, particularly when this assertion is uttered, as is always the case, upon the action of several initially merely soliciting and mutually exclusive motives. All of this taken together, then, is the source of the natural delusion which leads to the erroneous view that our self-consciousness contains the certainty of a freedom of our will, in the sense that, contrary to all laws of pure understanding and of nature, it determines itself without sufficient grounds, and that its resolves, under given circumstances and in one and the same man, could turn out in this way or in the opposite way.

In order to elucidate especially and most clearly the origination of this error, so important for our topic, and so to complete the investigation of the self-consciousness undertaken in the preceding section, let us imagine a man who, while standing on the street, would say to himself: "It is six o'clock in the evening, the working day is over. Now I can go for a walk, or I can go to the club; I can also climb up the tower to see the sun set; I can go to the theater; I can visit this friend or that one; indeed, I also can run out of the gate, into the wide world, and never return. All of this is strictly up to me, in this I have complete freedom. But still I shall do none of these things now, but with just as free a will I shall go home to my wife." This is exactly as if water spoke to itself: "I can make high waves (yes! in the sea during a storm), I can rush down hill (yes! in the river bed), I can plunge down foaming and gushing (yes! in the waterfall), I can rise freely as a stream of water into the air (yes! in the fountain), I can, finally, boil away and disappear (yes! at a certain temperature); but I am doing none of these things now, and am voluntarily remaining quiet and clear water in the reflecting pond."

As the water can do all those things only when the determining causes operate for the one or the other, so that man can do what he imagines himself able to do not otherwise than on the same condition. Until the causes begin to operate, this is impossible for him; but then, he *must,* as the water must, as soon as it is placed in the corresponding circumstances. His error and in general the delusion, which arises here from his falsely interpreted self-consciousness, that he can do all these things at this moment, rests, strictly speaking, on the fact that in his imagination only *one* picture at a time can be present and that for the moment it excludes everything else. When he imagines a motive for one of those actions which he pro-

poses to himself as possible, he feels immediately its effect on
his will, which is thereby solicited. This, in technical language,
is called a *velleitas*. But then he thinks that he can raise this to
the status of a *voluntas,* that is, that he can perform the pro-
posed action. However, this is a delusion. For soon sober
realization would set in and remind him of motives which pull
in other directions or are contrary to the original one. And he
would see that the action does not take place. In such succes-
sive imaginings of different, mutually exclusive motives, con-
stantly accompanied by the inner "I can do what I will," the
will turns, as it were, like a weather vane on a well-greased
pivot and in a changeable wind, immediately toward any
motive which imagination holds before it, and then in turn
toward all of the motives which appear possible. In the case of
each motive the man thinks that he can will it and so can fix
the vane at this point, but this is sheer delusion. For his "I
can will this" is in reality hypothetical and carries with it the
additional clause, "if I did not prefer the other." But this
addition annuls that ability to will.

Let us return to that man whom we had engaged in a
deliberation at six o'clock. Suppose he noticed that I am
standing behind him, philosophizing about him, and disput-
ing his freedom to perform all those actions which are possible
to him. It could easily happen that, in order to refute me, he
would perform one of them. But then my denial and its effect
on his contentious spirit would have been precisely the motive
which forced him to do so. However, this motive would be
able to move him only to one or the other of the easier of the
above-mentioned actions, e.g., to go to the theater, but by no
means to the last-mentioned, namely, to run out into the wide
world; this motive would be far too weak for that. An equally
erroneous supposition is made by a person who, holding a
loaded pistol in his hand, thinks that he can shoot himself
with it. For this the mechanical instrument is of the least
importance; the main thing is an exceedingly strong and
therefore rare motive which has the tremendous power required to outweigh the love of life, or, more correctly, the

fear of death. Only after such a motive has entered in can he really shoot himself, and must do so; unless an even stronger countermotive, if such a one is at all possible, prevents the deed.

I can do what I will: I can, if I will, give everything I have to the poor and thus become poor myself—if I will! But I cannot will this, because the opposing motives have much too much power over me for me to be able to. On the other hand, if I had a different character, even to the extent that I were a saint, then I would be able to will it. But then I could not keep from willing it, and hence I would have to do so.

All of this is perfectly compatible with the "I can do what I will" of the self-consciousness, in which some unthinking philosophasters claim even today to see the freedom of the will, and, accordingly, assert it as a given fact of consciousness. Among these Mr. Cousin distinguishes himself and therefore deserves an honorable mention here. In his *Cours d'histoire de la philosophie,* he teaches that the freedom of the will is the most reliable fact of consciousness and censures Kant for having proved it only from the moral law and having set it up only as a postulate, since according to Cousin it is a fact: "Why prove what it is sufficient to state?—Freedom is a fact, and not a belief." [4]

Meanwhile, in Germany too there is no shortage of igno-ramuses who throw to the winds all that has been said about this by great thinkers in the last 200 years, and, relying upon the fact of self-consciousness—analyzed in the preceding section and falsely interpreted by them as well as by the great mass—proclaim the freedom of the will as actually given. But perhaps I am unfair to them, as it may be the case that they are not as ignorant as they seem but only hungry, and there-fore, for a very dry piece of bread, teach everything that might please a lofty ministry.

It is definitely neither a metaphor nor a hyperbole but a quite dry and literal truth that, as little as a ball on a billiard table can move before receiving an impact, so little can a man

[4] V. Cousin, *Cours d'histoire de la philosophie* (Paris: 1841), I, 52.

get up from his chair before being drawn or driven by a motive. But then his getting up is as necessary and inevitable as the rolling of a ball after the impact. And to expect that anyone will do something to which absolutely no interest impels him is the same as to expect that a piece of wood shall move toward me without being pulled by a string. Should a man, maintaining this view in a gathering, encounter an obstinate opposition, he would get out of the affair in the shortest time if he had another man call out suddenly in a loud and solemn voice: "The roof is falling in." This would bring his opponents to the insight that a motive is just as capable of driving people out of the house as is the most robust mechanical cause.

For man, like all objects of experience, is a phenomenon in time and space, and since the law of causality holds for all such a priori and consequently without exception, he too must be subject to it. This is asserted *a priori* by the pure understanding, confirmed by the analogy found throughout the whole of nature, and attested by the experience of every moment, provided one does not succumb to the delusion arising from the consideration that, as natural beings become more complicated in the process of rising to a higher and higher level, and as their receptivity rises and becomes refined—from the merely mechanical to the chemical, electrical, irritable, sensible, intellectual, and, finally, rational—the nature of the activating causes must also proceed *pari passu* and correspond on each level to the beings which are to be activated. Consequently the causes must also present themselves as less and less palpable and material, so that in the end they are no longer visible to the eye but can indeed be reached by the understanding, which in each particular case presupposes them with unshakable confidence and discovers them too upon proper scrutiny. For here the acting causes are raised to the level of mere thoughts struggling with other thoughts, until the most powerful of them becomes decisive and sets the man in motion. All of this takes place with just such a strict causality as when purely mechanical causes work on one another in a complicated combination and the calculated effect occurs without fail. The appearance of causelessness due to the invisibility of the cause is found just as much among the electrified particles of cork which jump around in all directions in a glass as in the movements of man; but the eye is not entitled to judge, only the understanding.

If freedom of the will were presupposed, every human action would be an inexplicable miracle—an effect without a cause. And if one is bold enough to imagine such a *liberum arbitrium indifferentiae,* he will soon realize that in this effort the understanding is really at a standstill; it has no form with which to think such a thing. For the principle of sufficient reason, the principle of thoroughgoing determination and dependence of phenomena on one another, is the most universal form of our cognitive faculty, which, according to the difference of its objects, itself takes on different forms. But here we are supposed to think something which determines without being determined, which depends on nothing, but on which the other depends. This other, without any necessity, and consequently without any ground, produces A now, whereas it could just as well produce B, or C, or D. Furthermore, it could do this absolutely, under the same circumstances, that is, without there being anything in A which would confer upon it a prerogative over B, C, or D (for this would be motivation, hence causality). Here we are led back to the concept of the absolutely accidental, posited in the very beginning. I repeat: in this case the understanding is really quite at a standstill, if only one can bring it to that.

However, let us now remind ourselves what a cause really is: an antecedent change which makes the following one necessary. No cause in the world ever brings about its effect all by itself, or produces it out of nothing. Rather there is something present every time on which it acts, and it produces a change merely at this particular time, in this place, and on this definite being. This change always corresponds to the nature of that being which, therefore, must already have the force to produce it. Thus every effect originates from two factors, an inner and an outer one, namely, from the original force of that which is being acted upon, and from the determining cause which forces the former to manifest itself in this case.

Every causality and every explanation based on it presupposes original force; therefore the explanation never explains everything but always leaves something inexplicable. We see this in the whole of physics and chemistry: their explanations always presuppose natural forces which express themselves in phenomena. All explanation rests on tracing back phenomena to these natural forces. A natural force itself is subject to no explanation but is the principle of all explanation. Similarly, it is itself not subject to causality but is precisely that which confers causality upon every cause, i.e., the ability to act. It is itself the common substratum of all effects of this kind and is present in each of them. Thus the phenomena of magnetism are traced back to an original force called electricity. Here the explanation rests; it gives only the conditions under which such a force manifests itself, that is, the causes which bring forth its action. The explanations of the motion of heavenly bodies presuppose gravitation as force, by virtue of which the particular causes operate so as to determine the course of heavenly bodies. The explanations of chemistry presuppose the secret forces which manifest themselves, in accordance with certain stoicheiometric relations, as elective affinities. It is on these that all stated effects finally depend, and they set in with great accuracy when the given causes produce them. Similarly, all the explanations of physiology presuppose the life force which reacts in a definite way to the inner and outer stimuli. And so it is everywhere throughout. Even the causes with which such an intelligible study as mechanics is concerned, such as thrust and pressure, presuppose impenetrability, cohesion, rigidity, hardness, inertia, weight, elasticity, and these, no less than those mentioned above, are unfathomable natural forces. So everywhere causes determine nothing more than the When and Where of the manifestations of original, inexplicable forces. Only when such forces are presupposed can we speak of them as causes, that is, as necessarily producing certain effects.

That which is the case in respect to cause in the narrowest sense and in respect to stimuli is no less true with respect to motives. This is so because motivation is not different in essentials from causality but is only a kind of it, namely, the causality which passes through the medium of cognition. Here too the cause calls forth only a manifestation of a force which cannot be traced back to further causes, and consequently cannot be further explained. But this force, here called the will, is known to us not only from the outside like the other natural forces, but, by virtue of the self-consciousness, also from the inside and immediately. Only under the presupposition that such a will exists and that, in any given case, it is of a definite nature do causes directed toward it take effect, which are here called motives. This particularly and individually constituted nature of the will, by virtue of which its reaction to the same motives in every man is different, makes up that which one calls his character and, what is more, because it is not known a priori but only through experience, the empirical character. It is by its means that, to start with, the way in which various motives affect the given man is determined. For it underlies all effects which motives call forth in the same way as the general natural forces underlie the effects called forth by causes in the narrowest sense, and as the life force underlies the effects of the stimuli. And, like the natural forces it too is original, unchangeable, and inexplicable. In animals it is different for each species, in men for each individual. Only in the very highest, cleverest animals does a noticeable individual character manifest itself, although with the decisive preponderance of the species character.

The character of man is: 1) *individual:* in every one it is different. To be sure, the character of the species lies at the basis of all; therefore the main characteristics are repeated in every one. However, here there is such a significant difference of degree, such a difference of combination and mutual modification of characteristics, that one can assume the moral difference of characters to equal that of the intellectual capabilities; which is to say a great deal. It is also assumed that both are without comparison greater than the bodily difference between giant and dwarf, Apollo and Thersites. Therefore the effect of the same motive on different people is quite different; as the sunlight gives to wax white color and to chloric silver black, so the heat makes wax soft, but clay hard. Therefore from the knowledge of motives alone one cannot predict the act; in addition one must also have precise knowledge of the character in question.

2) The character of man is *empirical:* only through experience can one get to know it. This applies not only to others, but also to oneself. Therefore we are often disappointed with ourselves, as we are with others, when we discover that we do not have this or that quality, like justice, selflessness, or courage, in as high a degree as we most indulgently supposed. Hence too, in any difficult choice our own resolve, like that of another person, remains a mystery to us until the choice has been actually made. Now we believe that it will go in this direction and now in that, depending on whether the mind holds this or that motive more clearly before the will and the motive tries out its power, in which processes that "I can do what I will" produces the illusion of the will's freedom. Finally the stronger motive asserts its power over the will, and the choice often turns out quite differently than we initially supposed.

Therefore, finally, no one can know how another, and even how he himself, will act in a definite situation, until he has been in it. Only after the test has been passed is he sure of the other, and only then of himself too. But then he *is* sure: proved friends, tested servants are trustworthy. In general, we treat a person whom we know well like any other thing with whose properties we have already become familiar, and we know in advance what can be expected of him and what cannot. He who has done something once will do it again, good or bad, should the situation recur. For this reason the man who needs some great, extraordinary help will turn to the person who has proved himself generous; and he who wants to hire a murderer will look around among the people who have already had blood on their hands. According to Herodotus' story (VII, 164), Gelo of Syracuse was forced to entrust a great sum of money to a man unconditionally and to have him take it abroad at his own full discretion. For this task he chose Cadmos, who had proved to be a man of rare, indeed unprecedented honesty and conscientiousness; and his trust was completely substantiated.

Likewise, it is only out of experience and from opportunities to observe that our acquaintance with ourselves derives, on which self-trust or mistrust is based. Depending on whether in a given instance we have shown prudence, courage, honesty, discretion, astuteness, or whatever else the case might require, or whether the lack of such virtues has come to light, we are, as a result of the acquaintance made with ourselves, subsequently either satisfied or dissatisfied with ourselves. Only an exact knowledge of his own empirical character gives a man that which is called an acquired character. That man possesses it who knows accurately his own qualities, good as well as bad, and thus knows for certain with what he can trust himself, what he can expect of himself, and what he cannot. While till now, because of his empirical character, he played his role naturally, he now plays it artistically and methodically, with firmness and grace, without ever, as one says, being untrue to his character. Whenever a man is untrue to his character he shows that he was mistaken about his own self.

3) The character of man is *constant:* it remains the same, throughout the whole of life. Under the changeable shell of his years, his relationships, and even his store of knowledge and opinions, there hides, like a crab under its shell, the identical and real man, quite unchangeable and always the same. Only in respect to direction and content does his character undergo apparent modifications, which are the result of differences in one's age in life and its needs. Man never

changes; as he has acted in one case, so he will always act again—given completely equal circumstances (which, however, includes also the correct knowledge of those circumstances). A confirmation of this truth can be gathered from everyday experience. But one encounters it in the most striking manner when after twenty or thirty years one meets an acquaintance again and soon catches him doing the same silly things as formerly.

It is true that many a man will deny this truth in words, but still such a man presupposes it in his actions. Finding a man dishonest once, he never trusts him again, but he readily relies on the one who has proved himself honest in the past. For on this truth rests the possibility of all knowledge of human beings, and of the firm trust in those that are tested, tried out, and confirmed. Even when such a trust has once disappointed us, we never say: "His character has changed," but "I was mistaken about him." This truth is also the basis of the fact that when we want to determine the moral worth of an action, we make a special effort to be sure about its motive, but then our praise or blame is not aimed at the motive but at the character which allowed itself to be determined by such a motive, the character being the second and the only factor in this act which inheres in the man himself.

On the same truth rests the fact that when true honor (not the knightly or fool's honor) is once lost, it can never be regained: the stain of a single unworthy action sticks to a man forever, branding him, as the saying goes. Hence the proverb: "Whoever steals once, remains a thief all his life."

It is due to this truth that when, as may happen in important state affairs, a treason is planned and one hires a traitor, uses and rewards him, then, after the objective is obtained, it is wise to remove the traitor because whereas the circumstances are changeable, his character is not.

On this truth it rests that the greatest mistake of a dramatic poet is this, that his characters are not stable; that is, unlike those characters presented by great poets, they are not carried out with the constancy and strict consistency of a natural force, as I have shown to be the case by means of an extensive example from Shakespeare in my *Parerga*.[5]

Indeed, on the same truth rests the possibility of conscience, insofar as it holds up to us even in old age the misdeeds of our youth. This happened, for example, to J. J. Rousseau, who was reminded by his conscience after forty years that he had accused the maid Marion of a theft which he himself had committed. This is possible only on the assumption that the character has remained the same without change. On the other hand, the most ridiculous mistakes, the crudest ignorance, and the oddest stupidities of our youth do not make us feel ashamed in old age, for things have changed and those things were a matter of knowledge; we got away from them, put them away long ago, like our youthful clothing.

The same truth underlies the fact that a man, even in the clearest knowledge and indeed disgust at his moral failures and defects, and in the most sincere intention to reform, still does not really reform but, in spite of serious intentions and honest promises, and to his own surprise, finds himself, when the opportunity recurs, again treading the same paths as before. What can be corrected is only his knowledge, from which he can come to see that this or that means which he used before does not lead to his goal, or brings more loss than gain; then he changes the means, not the ends. This is the basis of the American penal system: it does not undertake to improve the character, the heart of a man. What it does attempt is to straighten him out and to show him that he would attain the goals which he irrevocably pursues by virtue of his character with much greater difficulty, hardships, and dangers by the route of dishonesty hereto followed than by the route of honesty, work, and contentedness.

Anyway, it is in cognition alone that the sphere and realm of improvement and ennobling is found. The character is unchangeable, and motives operate of necessity; however, they must pass through cognition, which is the medium of the

[5] [Vol. II, § 118, p. 196 of the first edition (2nd edition, § 119, p. 248). —Tr.]

motives. The cognition is capable of the most varied enlargement, of constant correction, in innumerable gradations. That is the goal of all education. The development of reason through information and insights of all kinds is morally important because it provides access for motives to which a man would otherwise remain inaccessible. As long as he could not understand them, they were not present for his will. Therefore, under the same external circumstances the situation of a man can actually be quite different the second time from what it was the first, provided that he has been able in the meantime to comprehend those circumstances correctly and completely, so that motives to which he formerly was inaccessible will act on him now. In this sense the scholastics spoke very truly: "The final cause (goal, motive) acts not according to its zeal, but according to its cognized essence." [6]

But no moral influence can reach further than the correction of cognition, and the undertaking to remove the failings of character of a man by means of talk and moralizing and thus to reform his character itself, his essential morality, is exactly like the attempt to change lead into gold by external action, or by means of careful cultivation to make an oak produce apricots.

The conviction that the unalterability of character is beyond the possibility of doubt we find expressed already by Apuleius in his *Oratio de magia* in which, defending himself against the charge of sorcery, he falls back upon his well-known character and says: "There is a sure proof in the character of every man which always naturally predisposes him in the same manner toward virtue or vice and is a sure basis for committing a crime or for avoiding it." [7]

4) The individual character is *inborn;* it is not a work of

___

[6] [*Causa finalis movet non secundum suum esse reale, sed secundum esse cognitum.* According to Deussen, Schopenhauer's editor, Schopenhauer said that the phrase *causa finalis* occurred in Suarez, *Disp. metaph.,* XXIII, sec. 7 and 8; however, Deussen failed to find the cited passage.—Tr.]

[7] [Apuleius, *The Works of Apuleius* (London: 1853).—Tr.]

art or of accidental circumstances, but the work of nature itself. It manifests itself already in the child and shows there on a small scale what it will be in the future on a large one. Hence two children who have exactly the same upbringing and surroundings will most clearly exhibit fundamentally different characters, characters which they will still have as old men. In its basic features character is even hereditary, but only on the father's side, while intelligence is inherited from the mother. Concerning this question I refer the reader to Chapter XLIII of the second volume of my main work.

From this presentation of the nature of individual character it follows of course that virtues and vices are inborn. This truth may be inconvenient to some prejudices and some old wives' philosophy, with its so-called practical interests, that is, its petty, narrow concepts and limited school-children views, but it was already the conviction of the father of morality, Socrates, who according to Aristotle maintained: "Being virtuous or vicious is not a matter of our choice." [8] What Aristotle maintains to the contrary here is evidently bad: for he also shares this opinion of Socrates and expresses it most clearly in the *Nicomachean Ethics:* "For all men think that each type of character belongs to its possessors in some sense by nature; for from the very moment of birth we are just or fitted for self-control or have the other moral qualities." [9]

If we survey all the virtues and vices in Aristotle's book *On Virtues and Vices,* where they are reviewed briefly, we shall find that in actual people all of them can be thought of only as inborn traits, and only as such can they be authentic. If on the other hand they came from reflection and were arbitrarily assumed, they would really amount to a sort of dissimulation; they would be unauthentic. Also for this reason we could not count at all on their permanence and reliability under pressure of circumstances.

When we consider in addition the Christian virtue of love, *caritas*—which is absent in Aristotle and in all ancients—the

8 [Aristotle, *Magna Moralia* (tr. W. D. Ross), I, 9, 1187a, 7.—Tr.]

9 [Aristotle, *Nicomachean Ethics* (tr. W. D. Ross), VI, 13, 1144b, 4.—Tr.]

matter is no different. How could the untiring goodness of one man and the incorrigible, deeply rooted wickedness of another—say the character of the Antonines, Hadrian, or Titus on the one hand, and that of Caligula, Nero, or Domitian on the other—alight upon them from the outside, be the work of accidental circumstances, or of mere knowledge and teaching? Didn't Nero have Seneca for a tutor? It is rather the case that the germ of all virtues and vices lies in the inborn character, in that real core of the whole man. This conviction, so natural to an unsophisticated man, guided also the hand of Valleius Paterculus as he wrote the following about Cato: "He resembled virtue herself, and in all his acts he revealed a character nearer to that of gods than of men. He never did a right action solely for the sake of seeming to do the right, but because he could not do otherwise." [10]

On the other hand, if one assumes the freedom of the will, it is absolutely impossible to say what is the source both of virtue and of vice, or of the fact that two men who were brought up in the same way act quite differently, indeed in an opposite way, under entirely equal circumstances and occasions. The actual, original, basic difference of the characters is incompatible with the assumption of a freedom of the will which means that for any man, in any situation, two contrary actions are equally possible. For then his character must be by nature a *tabula rasa*, like Locke's intellect, and can have no inborn tendency in one direction or another, since this

[10] [Velleius Paterculus, *Res Gestae Divi Augusti* (London, New York: 1924), p. 125, trans. Shipley.—Tr.] This passage is gradually becoming a standard weapon in the arsenal of the determinists, an honor of which the good old historian, 1800 years ago, certainly never dreamed. First it was praised by Hobbes, and after him by Priestley. Then it was quoted by Schelling in his treatise on freedom [F. W. J. v. Schelling, "Ueber das Wesen der menschlichen Freiheit," *Schellings Werke* (Leipzig: 1907), III, 489.—Tr.], in a translation somewhat falsified for his purposes; for which reason he does not name Valleius Paterculus directly, but, with equal shrewdness and elegance, says, "an ancient." Finally, I also did not want to miss the opportunity to quote it, since it really is relevant here.

would indeed eliminate that complete equilibrium which one thinks of in the *liberum arbitrium indifferentiae*. Hence, when this is assumed, the basis of the difference in the manner in which different people act cannot be found in the subjective aspect. But even less can it be found in the objective aspect, for then the *objects* would determine action, and the required freedom would be completely lost. Then at best only this way out would be left, namely to locate the origin of that truly great difference in behavior in a middle ground between subject and object, that is, to regard it as arising from the different ways in which the objective is grasped by the subjective, or as it was cognized by different people. But then everything would revert to a correct or incorrect knowledge of the given circumstances, whereby the moral difference in behavior would be transformed into a mere difference of the correctness of judgment, and morality would be transformed into logic.

If now the adherents of the freedom of the will should try to get out of that difficult dilemma by saying that there is indeed no inborn difference of characters but that such a difference arises from external circumstances, impressions, experiences, examples, teachings, etc.—and if a character had come into being for once in this way, the difference of behavior could be subsequently explained from that—then we must reply, first, that according to this view the character would put in an appearance very late (whereas actually it can already be recognized in children) and that most people would die before having attained a character; and second, that all those external circumstances whose effect the character was supposed to be lie completely outside of our power and would be brought about in one or the other way by chance (or, if one prefers, by Providence). Now, if it is from these that the character and from this in turn the difference of behavior arises, then all moral responsibility for the latter would completely disappear, since obviously this difference would ultimately be the work of chance or of Providence.

Thus, when the freedom of the will is assumed, we see that the origin of the difference in behavior, and therewith of virtue or vice, together with responsibility, floats adrift and nowhere finds a place to take root. From this it is evident that this assumption, no matter how much it suits the untutored understanding at first sight, contradicts at bottom our moral convictions as much as it does the highest principle of our understanding, as has been sufficiently proved.

As I have shown above in detail, the necessity with which the motives—like all causes in general—operate, is not without presuppositions. We have now learned its presupposition, the basis and the ground on which it rests: it is the inborn individual character. As every effect in inanimate nature is a necessary product of two factors, namely, of the general natural force which manifests itself here and of the particular cause which calls forth this manifestation, just so every action of a man is the necessary product of his character and of the operating motive. Given both of them, the effect follows inevitably. For a different action to occur, either a different motive or a different character would have to be posited. Moreover, one could predict with assurance, indeed calculate, every action, were it not for the fact that on the one hand the character is very difficult to fathom, and on the other hand the motive is frequently hidden and always exposed to the countereffect of other motives which lie only in the sphere of the one man's thought, inaccessible to others.

The inborn character of a man determines in essentials even the goals toward which he unalterably strives: the means which he takes for this purpose are determined partly by the external circumstances and partly by his conception of them. The correctness of his conception depends in turn on his understanding and education. His particular actions take place as the end product of all of this, and so does the entire role which he plays in the world. The conclusion of the doctrine of the individual character, as presented here, finds an expression as accurate as it is poetic, in one of Goethe's most beautiful stanzas:

Wie an dem Tag, der dich der Welt verliehen,
Die Sonne stand zum Grusse der Planeten,
Bist alsobald und fort und fort gediehen,
Nach dem Gesetz, wonach du angetreten.
So musst du sein, dir kannst du nicht entfliehen,
So sagten schon Sibyllen, so Propheten;
Und keine Zeit und keine Macht zerstückelt
Geprägte Form, die lebend sich entwickelt.[11]

Thus that assumption on which the necessity of the operations of *all* causes rests is the inner being of every thing—be it merely a general natural force which manifests itself in it, or be it life force, or be it will. In every case the particular being, of whatever type, will react according to its special nature, whenever causes act upon it. This law, to which all things in the world are subject without exception, was expressed by the scholastics in the formula *operari sequitur esse.* According to it, the chemist tests substances by means of reagents, and a man tries out another man by means of tests which he applies to him. In all cases the external causes will necessarily call forth that which is hidden in a being; for this being cannot react otherwise than according to its nature.

Here one must be reminded that every existence presupposes an essence, that is, every thing-in-being must be *something,* must have a definite nature. It cannot exist and yet be nothing, it cannot be something like the *ens metaphysicum,* that is, a thing which simply *is* and no more than *is,* without any definitions and properties, and consequently, without a definite way of acting which flows from them. As little as an essence yields a reality without an existence (as Kant expounded in the familiar example of the 100 talers), just as

11 [Goethe, "Orphisch":

As on the day that gave you to the earth,
The sun greeted the planets in their course,
You, likewise, grew and throve, and from your birth
Followed the law that was your primal source.
So must you be, your self you can't escape,
This said the sibyls, this the prophets hold;
And time and might are powerless to break
Predestined form, that living things unfold.

(translated by Edythe Fulton).]

little can an existence do this without an essence. For every thing-in-being must have a nature which is essential and peculiar to it, in virtue of which it is what it is, which this being always maintains, and whose manifestations are called forth of necessity by causes; while on the other hand this nature itself is by no means the effect of those causes, nor can it be modified by them. But all this is just as true of man and his will as of all other beings in nature. He too has an essence in addition to existence, that is, fundamental properties which make up his character and require only an outside inducement in order to reveal themselves. Consequently, to expect that a man should act one time in one way, another time quite differently, in response to the same cause, would be no different than to expect that the same tree which bore cherries this summer should bear pears in the next. Freedom of the will, when carefully analyzed, means an existence without an essence, which means that something *is* and at the same time *is nothing,* which in turn means *is not,* and consequently is a self-contradiction.

The insight into this truth as well as into the a priori certain and therefore exceptionless validity of the law of causality accounts for the fact that all really deep thinkers of all times, no matter how different their other views may have been, agreed in maintaining the necessity of volitions upon the occurrence of motives, and in rejecting the *liberum arbitrium.* Precisely because the incalculably great majority of the masses, incapable of thought and victims of illusion and prejudice, were always stubbornly opposed to this truth, those thinkers have given this truth the highest prominence in order to propound it in the most definite, indeed most frolicsome assertions. The best known of these is the story of Buridan's ass, for which, however, men have sought in vain for a hundred years in the still available writings of Buridan. I myself possess an edition of his *Sophismata,* apparently printed in the 15th century, without indication of the place of printing or of the year, and without page numbering. I have often searched for that illustration in this book, but in vain, despite the fact that on almost every page asses are referred to as examples. Bayle, whose article *Buridan* is the basis of everything that was written subsequently, says quite incorrectly that one knows only about one sophism of Buridan; I myself have a whole quarto of his sophisms. Since Bayle has treated the matter so extensively he should have known—which, however, seems to have remained unnoticed ever since his time —that the example, which in a way has become a symbol or type of the great truth which I am here defending, is much older than Buridan. It can be found in Dante, who possessed the entire store of knowledge of his time, who lived before Buridan, and who speaks not of asses but of men, in the following words, opening the fourth book of his *Paradise:*

> "Between two foods, each near in like degree
> And tempting, would a man starve ere he chose
> To put one to his teeth, though choice were free."

Indeed, it is already found in Aristotle, in these words: "The man who, though exceedingly hungry and thirsty, and both equally, yet being equidistant from food and drink, is therefore bound to stay where he is." [12] Buridan, who had taken over the example from these sources, exchanged man for an ass, merely because it was the habit of this paltry scholastic to use as his examples either Socrates and Plato or an ass.

The question of the freedom of the will is really a touchstone by which one can distinguish the deeply thinking minds from the superficial ones, or it is a milestone at which their ways part, all the former maintaining the necessary occurrence of an action when the character and the motive are given, and the latter, together with the great masses, clinging to the freedom of the will. There is also a type of a middle-of-the-roader who, feeling embarrassed, tacks back and forth, shifts the target for himself and others, hides behind words and phrases, or turns and twists the question so long that one no longer knows what it amounted to. This was what Leibniz did, who was much more of a mathematician and a learned

[12] [Aristotle, *De Coelo*, II, 12, 295b, 32.—Tr.]

man than a philosopher.[13] But in order to make such vacillating talkers face the question, one must put it to them in
the following way and insist that they answer it.

1) To a given man under given circumstances, are two actions possible, or only one?—The answer of all who think
deeply: only one.

2) Let us consider that a man's character remains unchanged and also that the circumstances whose influence he
had to experience were necessarily determined throughout
and down to the least detail by external causes, which always
take place with strict necessity and whose chain, entirely consisting of likewise necessary links, continues into infinity.
Could the completed life course of such a man turn out in
any respect, even the smallest, in any happening, any scene,
differently from the way it did?—No! is the consistent and correct answer.

The conclusion from both propositions is: Everything that
happens, from the largest to the smallest, happens necessarily.
Quidquid fit necessario fit.

Anyone who is frightened by these propositions has still to
learn some things and unlearn others. But then he will realize
that they are the most abundant source of comfort and tran-
quility. Our acts are indeed not a first beginning; therefore
nothing really new comes through them into being. But this
is true: *through that which we do we only find out what we
are.*

On the conviction of the strict necessity of all that happens,
a conviction not clearly recognized and yet felt, rests also the
concept of fate or destiny which was so firmly held by the
ancients. So does the fatalism of the Mohammedans, and even
the ineradicable belief in omens. This is so because even the
smallest accident happens necessarily and all occurrences, so
to speak, keep time with one another, so that everything
reverberates in everything else. Finally, connected with this

[13] Leibniz' want of principle in this matter shows itself most clearly
in his letter to Coste, *Opera phil.*, ed. Erdmann, p. 447, and later also in
Theodicy, p. 45-53.

is even the fact that a man who has crippled or killed another without the slightest intention, or quite accidentally, regrets this misfortune throughout the rest of his life with a feeling which seems akin to that of guilt. Moreover, as a *persona piacularis* (unfortunate person) he finds in the eyes of others a peculiar kind of discredit. Indeed, the felt conviction of the unchangeability of character and the necessity of its manifestation was probably not without an influence even on the Christian doctrine of election by grace.

Finally, I do not want to suppress still another incidental observation, which anyone may either accept or reject, according to the way he thinks about some matters. If we do not accept the strict necessity of all that happens by means of a causal chain which connects all events without exception, but allow this chain to be broken in countless places by an absolute freedom, then all foreseeing of the future, in dreams, in clairvoyant somnambulism, second sight, becomes objective and hence absolutely impossible, and so inconceivable. Because then there is no objectively real future which could possibly be foreseen, but instead of saying this we merely doubt the subjective conditions, hence the subjective possibility of this foresight. Even this doubt can no longer be entertained today by the well-informed, after innumerable testimonies of the most trustworthy kind have established those anticipations of the future.

Let me add just a few more considerations as corollaries to the established doctrine of the necessity of all that happens.

What would become of this world if necessity did not permeate all things and hold them together, but especially govern the procreation of individuals? A monster, a rubbish heap, a caricature without sense and meaning—namely, the work of a true and real chaos.

To wish that some event had not taken place is a silly self-torture, for this means to wish something absolutely impossible, and is as irrational as is the wish that the sun should rise in the West. Precisely because everything that happens, great or small, happens with strict necessity, it is altogether useless to reflect on how insignificant and accidental were the causes which brought that event about, and how easily they could have been different. For this is illusory. All of them have happened with just as strict necessity and have done this work with just as full a power as that in virtue of which the sun rises in the East. We should rather consider the events, as they happen, with the same eye as we consider the printed word which we read, knowing full well that it was there before we read it.

◦◎ؤ IV ◎◦

PREDECESSORS

In support of the above claim about the judgment of all those who reflected deeply on our problem let me remind the reader of some of the great men who have expressed themselves to this effect.

First of all, to calm those who might think that religious considerations conflict with the truth which I am defending, I would like to remind them that Jeremiah said long ago, "The way of man is not in himself, it is not in man who walks to direct his steps." [1] But in particular I would like to appeal to Luther, who disputes the freedom of the will with all his vehemence in *De servo arbitrio,* the book which he wrote especially for that purpose. A few passages from it will suffice to characterize his views, which he naturally supports not with philosophical but with theological considerations:

Therefore we find it written in all hearts equally that free will is nothing; even though this conviction is obscured by so many assertions to the contrary and by various authorities.—Here I should like to ask the defenders of free will to bear in mind that with their free will they are denying Christianity.—All testimonies (of the Scripture) which deal with Christ oppose the freedom of the will. These are innumerable, indeed the whole of Scripture deals with Him. Hence, if we take the Scripture to be the judge in this case, then I shall be entirely vindicated in my view that there remains not a single iota or a dash which does not condemn the doctrine of free will. [2]

Now let us turn to philosophers. Here the ancients are not to be taken into serious consideration, since their philosophy,

[1] [Jeremiah, 10:23.—Tr.]

[2] Martin Luther, *On the Bondage of the Will.* Schopenhauer quotes from the Schmidt edition of Luther's works, Strassburg, 1707, pp. 145, 214, 220.—Tr.]

still in the innocent stage, as it were, had not yet brought the two deepest and most delicate problems of modern philosophy to clear consciousness, namely, the problem of the freedom of the will and that of the reality of the external world, or of the relation between the ideal and the real. The extent, by the way, to which the problem of the freedom of the will had become clear to the ancients can be pretty well discerned from Aristotle's *Nicomachean Ethics* (III, 1-8), where we find that his thinking about this problem concerns itself in essentials only with physical and intellectual freedom. This is why he speaks only of the voluntary and the involuntary, taking "voluntary" and "free" as equivalent in meaning. The much more difficult problem of moral freedom had not yet occurred to him, although, to be sure, at times his thoughts penetrate that far, especially in the *Nicomachean Ethics* (II, 2 and III, 7), where, however, he commits the mistake of deducing the character from the acts, instead of the reverse. Similarly, he falsely criticizes Socrates' conviction which I have quoted above; but in other places he made it his own, as in the *Nicomachean Ethics* (X, 10): "Nature's part evidently does not depend on us, but as a result of some divine causes is present in those who are truly fortunate." "The character, then, must somehow be there already with a kinship to virtue, loving what is noble and hating what is base." [3] This agrees with the passage I cited above, as also with *Magna Moralia*, (I, 11): "For he who wills to be best will not be so, unless Nature also be presupposed; better, however, he will be." [4]

Aristotle treats the problem of the freedom of the will in the same sense in *Magna Moralia*, (I, 9-18) and *Ethica Eudemia* (II, 6-10), where he comes still a little closer to the real problem. Nevertheless even there everything is hesitant and superficial. His method everywhere is not to go to the problem directly, by analytical procedure; instead, he draws conclusions synthetically, from external features. Instead of pushing through in order to get to the heart of the matter,

[3] [Aristotle, *Nicomachean Ethics*, X, 10, 1179b, 21.—Tr.]
[4] [Aristotle, *Magna Moralia*, I, 11, 1187b, 28.—Tr.]

he keeps to the external earmarks, even words. This method misleads easily, and in the case of deeper problems never leads to the goal. Aristotle stops before the supposed opposition between the necessary and the voluntary, as if before a wall. But only beyond this wall lies the insight that the voluntary, just as such, is necessary, by virtue of the motive without which volition is no more possible than without a subject who wills. Besides, such a motive is a cause, as much as a mechanical one is, from which it differs only in inessential detail. He himself says: "the object of an action is one of the causes." [5] Therefore that opposition between the voluntary and the necessary is fundamentally false, though many alleged philosophers even today still repeat Aristotle's mistake.

The problem of the freedom of the will is already presented rather clearly by Cicero in the book *De Fato* (Chapters X and XVII). The subject matter of his treatise leads up to it, to be sure, very easily and naturally. He himself is on the side of the freedom of the will. But we see that Chrysippus and Diodoros must already have become aware of the problem, more or less clearly. Worthy of notice is also the thirtieth funeral oration of Lucian, between Minos and Sostratos, which denies the freedom of the will and with it responsibility.

The fourth book of the Maccabees in the Septuagint (in Luther it is absent) is in a way a treatise on the freedom of the will, insofar as it sets itself the task of proving that reason has the power to overcome all passions and affections, and documents this by the Jewish martyrs in the second book.

The earliest clear knowledge of our problem, as far as I know, appears in Clement of Alexandria, who says: "Neither praise nor blame, neither paying a tribute nor punishment would be justified, if the soul did not have the capacity for striving or resistance, if wickedness were involuntary." [6] And then, in a parenthetical remark referring to a previous statement: "So that God is even less responsible for our wicked-

[5] [Aristotle, *Ethica Eudemia*, II, 10, 1226b, 26.–Tr.]

[6] [Clement of Alexandria, *Stromata*, I, chap. XVII, § 83.–Tr.]

ness." [7] This most noteworthy postscript shows in what sense the church at once grasped the problem, and what decision, from its own interest, it immediately anticipated.

Almost two hundred years later we find the doctrine of free will extensively treated by Nemesius, in his work *On Human Nature* (Chapter XXXV, at the end, and Chapters XXXIX-XLI). The freedom of the will is here simply identified with voluntariness, or decision in choosing, and most zealously maintained and demonstrated in that sense. Yet at least the matter is already being aired.

But the fully developed awareness of our problem, together with all that depends on it, we find for the first time in the church father Augustine. For this reason, though more a theologian than a philosopher, he is important here. We see at once that this problem gets him into noticeable embarrassment and uncertain wavering, leading him to inconsistencies and contradictions in his three books, *On Free Will*. On the one hand, he does not want, as does Pelagius, to concede so much to the freedom of the will that original sin, the need of salvation, and the free election by grace would be eliminated. This would make man righteous through his own power and worthy of salvation. He even lets us understand [8] that he would have said still more on this side of the controversy (for which Luther later fought so vehemently), had not those books been written before the emergence of Pelagius, against whose views he then wrote *Of Nature and Grace*. Meanwhile he already says: "Because he is what he now is, he is not good, nor is it in his power to become good, either because he does not see what he ought to be, or, seeing it, he has not the power to be what he sees he ought to be." [9] And again: "Nor is it any wonder either that because of ignorance man has not a free judgment of will for choosing what he should rightly do; or that by the opposition of carnal habit, which by the force of the mortal succession has become a sort of second nature, man

[7] [*Ibid.,* § 84.—Tr.]

[8] [Augustine, *On Free Will,* Book I, chap. IX.—Tr.]

[9] [Augustine, *On Free Will,* Book III, chap. XVIII.—Tr.]

sees what he should rightly do, and wants to do it, but cannot accomplish it." [10] And in the above-mentioned *On Free Will:* "But mortals cannot live righteously and piously unless the will itself is liberated by the grace of God from the servitude to sin into which it has fallen, and is aided to overcome its vices." [11]

On the other hand, the following three reasons moved him to defend the freedom of the will:

1) His opposition to the Manicheans, against whom the books *On Free Will* are explicitly directed, because they denied free will and assumed a different source of both wickedness and evil. To them he alludes already in the last chapter of the book *On the Quantity of Soul:* "Man is granted free choice, and he who tries to shake it by farcical sophistry, is so blind that he, etc." [12]

2) The natural delusion which I have laid bare and because of which the "I can do what I will" is regarded as the freedom of the will and "voluntary" is immediately identified with "free." "For what more truly lies within the will than the will itself?" [13]

3) The need to harmonize the moral responsibility of man with God's justice. The penetrating intelligence of Augustine did not fail to notice a most serious difficulty, which is so hard to remove that, as far as I know, all later philosophers with the exception of three, whom for this reason we shall soon examine more closely, have preferred to steal around it quietly, as if it did not exist. But Augustine utters it with noble sincerity in a quite straightforward fashion right in the introductory words of his books *On Free Will:* "Tell me, pray, whether God is not the author of evil?" [14] And then more extensively in the second chapter: "But the mind is troubled by the problem: if sins come from the souls which God has

10 [*Ibid.*—Tr.]
11 [*Ibid.*—Tr.]
12 [Augustine, *De Animae Quantitate.*—Tr.]
13 [Augustine, *On Free Will*, I, chap. XII, § 26.—Tr.]
14 [*Ibid.*, chap. I, § 1.—Tr.]

created, and those souls are from God, how comes it that sins
are not, at a slight remove, to be thrown back upon God?" [15]
To this the interlocutor replies: "Now you have put clearly
what I have been racking my brain to think out." [16]

This highly dubious consideration was taken up again by
Luther and brought out with the full force of his eloquence:

> But that God must be such that he subjects us to necessity
> in virtue of his freedom, even natural reason must admit.—
> If we grant that God is omniscient and omnipotent, then
> it follows obviously and incontestably that we did not create
> ourselves, do not live nor do anything through ourselves,
> but only through his omnipotence.—God's omniscience and
> omnipotence are diametrically opposed to the freedom of
> our will.—All men are inevitably compelled to admit that
> we become what we are not through our will but through
> necessity, that we therefore cannot do what we please in
> virtue of a freedom of will, but rather do what God has
> foreseen and brings about through inevitable and irrevoca-
> ble decision and will.[17]

Entirely filled with this insight was Vanini, who lived in the
beginning of the seventeenth century. It is the heart and the
soul of his persistent revolt against theism, even though this
revolt had to be concealed as slyly as possible because of the
pressure of the times. At every opportunity he comes back to
this insight and does not weary of presenting it from the most
varied points of view. For instance, in his *Amphitheatre of
Eternal Providence* he says:

> If God wills the sins, he brings them about, for it is written:
> "whatever he wills, he brings about." If he does not will
> them and they are nevertheless committed, then we must
> say of him that he either does not have foresight, or is not
> omnipotent, or is cruel; for he either does not know how to
> execute his decisions, or is impotent, or is negligent.—Phi-
> losophers say: if God did not want wicked and base actions
> to occur in the world, he undoubtedly would have extermi-

15 [*Ibid.*, chap. II, § 4.—Tr.]
16 [*Ibid.*, § 5.—Tr.]
17 [Luther, *op. cit.*, p. 144.—Tr.]

nated and banished from the world all shameful acts with one nod. For who of us could resist God's will? How can crimes be committed contrary to God's will if in each sinful act he provides the transgressor with the power to commit this act? Furthermore, if man sets himself against God's will, God is inferior to man who opposes him and prevails. From this it follows that God wills the world the way it is, and that if he had willed a better world he would have had a better one." [18]

And in Exercise 44 we have the following:

The instrument always follows the direction imposed on it by its owner; and since our will in actions is no more than an instrument, while God is the principal agent, it follows that God is responsible for the errors of the will.—Our will depends on God entirely, not only in respect to all its actions but also in respect to its essence. So that there is nothing for which one could hold the will responsible—be it in its action or in its essence—but everything must be imputed to God who has thus created the will and set it in motion.— Since the essence and the activity of will stem from God, all operations of the will, good or bad, must be attributed to him, the will being no more than an instrument in his hands. [19]

But in Vanini's case one must keep in mind that he employs throughout the strategy of putting into the mouth of his opponents his own actual opinion as the one which he abhors and wants to refute. Consequently, he presents it convincingly and thoroughly, to turn against it, in his own person, with shallow reasons and shaky arguments. Then, as if he had done his job well, he retreats triumphantly, relying on the malignity of his reader. By means of this craftiness he fooled the highly learned Sorbonne, which, taking all of this for true coin, candidly put the stamp of approval on his most godless writings. The more gladly three years later did it see him burnt alive, but not before his God-blaspheming tongue had been cut out. This is namely the really strong argument of

[18] [Vanini, *Amphitheatrum Aeternae Providentiae*, Exercitatio 16.—Tr.]
[19] [*Ibid.*, Exercitatio 44.—Tr.]

the theologians, and since it has been taken from them, things have been going backwards very fast.

If I am not mistaken, Hume is the first among the philosophers in the stricter sense who did not steal around the weighty difficulty first raised by Augustine, but put it forward without concealment in his essay *On Liberty and Necessity*, without, however, taking into account Augustine or Luther, to say nothing of Vanini. There, toward the end, it is written:

> The ultimate author of all our volitions is the creator of the world, who first bestowed motion on this immense machine, and placed all beings in that particular position, whence every subsequent event, by an inevitable necessity, must result. Human actions therefore either can have no turpitude at all, as proceeding from so good a cause; or, if they have any turpitude, they must involve our creator in the same guilt, while he is acknowledged to be their ultimate cause and author. For a man, who fired a mine, is answerable for all the consequences, whether the train employed be long or short; so wherever a continued chain of necessary causes is fixed, that being, either finite or infinite, who produces the first, is likewise the author of all the rest.[20]

He makes an attempt to solve this difficulty, but confesses at the end that he holds it to be insoluble.

Kant also, independently of his predecessors, hit upon the same stumbling block in the *Critique of Practical Reason:*

> It nevertheless appears that as soon as it is assumed that God as the Universal Primordial Being is the cause also of the existence of substance, one must also grant that the actions of a man have their determining ground in something completely beyond his own power, i.e., in the causality of a Highest Being which is different from him and upon which his existence and the entire determination of his causality absolutely depend.—Man would be a marionette or an automaton like Vaucanson's, fabricated and wound up by the Supreme artist; self-consciousness would indeed make him a thinking automaton, but the consciousness of his spontaneity, if this is held to be freedom, would be a mere

[20] [David Hume, "Of Liberty and Necessity," *An Inquiry Concerning Human Understanding* (New York: 1955), chap. VIII, 90-111.—Tr.]

illusion. It would deserve to be called so only comparatively, as the proximate determining causes of its movement and a long series of their determining causes would be internal, while the ultimate and highest would lie wholly in a foreign hand.[21]

He then tries to remove this great difficulty by distinguishing between the thing-in-itself and appearance, but this so obviously fails to change anything essential in this matter that I am convinced he was not really serious on this point. He himself admits the inadequacy of his solution when he adds:

> But is any other solution, which anyone has attempted or may attempt, any easier or more comprehensible? Rather might we say that the dogmatic teachers of metaphysics have shown more shrewdness than frankness in removing this difficult point as far as possible from view in the hope that, if they did not speak of it, no one would be likely to think of it.[22]

After this very noteworthy compilation of most heterogeneous voices which all say the same thing, I return now to our church father. He felt the full weight of the difficulty, but was hoping to remove it by theological and not philosophical reasoning; hence this reasoning is not unconditionally valid. In addition to the two above-mentioned reasons why he tried to defend the *liberum arbitrium* granted to man by God, he supported his argument by a third one, as already indicated. Since such a *liberum arbitrium* would plant itself in the middle between the creator and the sins of his creature and separate them, it would be really adequate to remove the entire difficulty, if only, as it can easily be put in words and might possibly satisfy a thinking which does not go much beyond words, it could at least continue to be thinkable, even upon serious and fairly deep reflection. But how should one imagine that a being which in its entire existence and essence is the product

21 [Immanuel Kant, *Critique of Practical Reason* (New York: 1956), pp. 104-05, trans. L. W. Beck.—Tr.]

22 [*Ibid.*, pp. 106-07.—Tr.]

of something else can still determine itself originally and fundamentally and hence be responsible for its acts? This assumption is invalidated by the proposition *operari sequitur esse,* that is, the effects of every being follow from its nature, whereas this proposition itself cannot be invalidated.

If a man acts badly, it is due to the fact that he is bad. But that proposition has a corollary: as a thing is, so it acts (*ergo unde esse, inde operari*). What would one say of a watchmaker who was angry at his watch for not running properly? Try as we may to make the will a *tabula rasa,* we shall still have to admit that when, for instance, the behavior of one of two men is, morally speaking, quite the opposite of the behavior of the other, this difference must be somehow accounted for. Either it has its source in the external circumstances, and then the guilt obviously cannot be ascribed to men, or in an original difference of their wills. But if the latter is the case, that is, if their entire being and nature is an effect of another, then again guilt and merit cannot be attributed to them.

Seeing that the great men quoted above exerted themselves in vain to find a way out of this labyrinth, I willingly admit that it is also beyond my power to think of the moral responsibility of the human will without thinking of that will as self-determined. Undoubtedly it was the same inability that dictated the seventh of the eight definitions with which Spinoza begins his *Ethics:* "That thing is called free which exists from the necessity of its own nature alone and is determined to action by itself alone. That thing, on the other hand, is called necessary or rather compelled which by another is determined to existence and action in a fixed and prescribed manner." [23]

If a bad act arises from nature, that is, from the inborn constitution of man, then obviously the guilt rests with the originator of this nature; that is why free will was invented. But if free will is assumed, it is not at all clear from what this nature should arise, because basically free will is only a purely negative characteristic and merely asserts that nothing com-

[23] [Spinoza, *Ethics* (New York: 1949), I, def. 7, p. 41, ed. James Gutmann.—Tr.]

pels a man or prevents him from acting thus or so. And so the origin of an action remains forever unexplained, since it is not supposed to come from the inborn or acquired constitution of man—for then it would be the fault of the creator—nor from the external circumstances alone, for in that case it would have to be ascribed to accident. Man would thus remain blameless in either case; nevertheless he is made responsible for the action.

The natural illustration of a free will is an empty balance; it hangs there quietly and will never get out of equilibrium unless something is placed in one of the scales. As little as the balance can move by itself, so little can the free will bring forth an action on its own, simply because nothing comes from nothing. If the balance is to dip on one side, a foreign body must be placed on it, which is the source of the motion. Similarly, the human action must be brought forth by something which acts positively and is something more than a merely negative freedom. But this can only be one of two things: either it is done by the motives themselves, that is, by external circumstances, and then the man is obviously not responsible for the action and, furthermore, in that case all men would have to act in exactly the same way under the same circumstances. Or it arises from his receptivity to such motives, hence from his inborn character, in other words, from the inclinations which originally inhere in the man and can be different in different individuals, and by the force of which the motives take effect. But then the will is no longer free, for these inclinations are the weight which is placed on the scale pan. The responsibility falls back on the one who put them there, in other words, on the one who created man with such inclinations. Therefore, man is responsible for his actions only if he is his own creation, i.e., is self-determined.

The whole point of view which is here presented permits us to estimate the scope of the problems connected with the freedom of the will. This freedom creates an inevitable chasm between the creator and the sins of his creature. Thus it becomes understandable why the theologians hold on so tenaciously to the freedom of the will, and why their shield bearers, the professors of philosophy, dutifully support them in this enterprise with such a zeal that they, deaf and blind to the most convincing counterproofs of great thinkers, hold on to free will and fight for it, as if for home and altar (*pro ara et focis*).

But let me finally conclude my report on Augustine, interrupted above. On the whole his view adds up to this: in reality man had a completely free will only before the fall, but after it, now a victim of original sin, he must hope for his salvation through election by grace and redemption—which is to speak like a church father.

Meanwhile, thanks to Augustine and his controversy with the Manicheans and the Pelagians, philosophy woke up to the consciousness of our problem. From then on, thanks to the scholastics, the problem gradually became clearer to the philosophers, to which Buridan's sophism and the above cited passage from Dante testify. But the one who was the first to come to the heart of the matter was, to all appearances, Thomas Hobbes, whose work, dedicated precisely to this problem, *Questions of Liberty and Necessity*, appeared in 1656. This work is now rare. In English it can be found in Th. Hobbes's *Moral and Political Works*, from which I quote the following fundamental passage:

> 6) Nothing takes a beginning from *itself*; but from the action of some other immediate *agent*, without itself. Therefore, when first a man has an appetite or will to something, to which immediately before he had no *appetite* nor *will;* the *cause* of his *will* is not the will itself, but *something* else not in his own disposing. So that, whereas it is out of controversy, that of *voluntary* actions the *will* is the *necessary* cause, and by this which is said, the *will* is also necessarily *caused* by other things, whereof it disposes not, it follows that *voluntary* actions have all of them necessary causes, and therefore are necessitated.
>
> 7) I hold that to be a *sufficient cause*, to which nothing is wanting that is needful to the producing of the *effect*. The same is also a necessary cause: for, if it be possible that a sufficient cause shall not bring forth the *effect*, then there

wanteth somewhat, which was needful to the producing of it; and so the *cause* was not *sufficient.* But if it be impossible that a *sufficient* cause should not produce the *effect;* then is a sufficient cause a *necessary* cause.—Hence it is manifest, that whatever is produced, is produced *necessarily.* For whatsoever is produced has had a *sufficient* cause to produce it, or else it had not been: and therefore also *voluntary* actions are *necessitated.*

8) That ordinary *definition* of a *free agent* (namely *that a free agent is that, which, when all things are present, which are needfull to produce the* effect, *can nevertheless not produce it*) implies a contradiction and is Nonsense; being as much as to say, the cause may be *sufficient,* that is to say *necessary,* and yet the *effect* shall not follow.—

Every accident, how contingent soever it seem, or how voluntary soever it be, is produced necessarily.[24]

In his famous book *De Cive,* he says: "For every man is desirous of what is good for him, and shuns what is evil, but chiefly the chiefest of natural evils, which is death; and this he doth by a certain impulsion of nature, no less than that whereby a stone moves downward." [25]

Immediately after Hobbes we see Spinoza completely permeated by the same conviction. A few passages will be sufficient to characterize his teaching on this point.

The will cannot be called a free cause, but can only be called necessary.—For the will, like all other things, needs a cause by which it may be determined to (existence and) action in a certain manner.[26]

With regard to the fourth objection (about Buridan's ass), I say that I entirely grant that if a man were placed in such a state of equilibrium he would perish of hunger and thirst, supposing he perceived nothing but hunger and thirst, and the food and drink which were equidistant from him.[27]

---

[24] [Thomas Hobbes, "Of Liberty and Necessity," *The English Works of Thomas Hobbes* (London: 1840), IV, 274-75, 277.—Tr.]

[25] [*Ibid.,* II, 8.—Tr.]

[26] [Spinoza, *op. cit.,* I, prop. XXXII, coroll. 2, p. 67. Schopenhauer omitted the words "existence and" from the text.—Tr.]

[27] [*Ibid.,* II, prop. XLIX, p. 124.—Tr.]

These decrees of the mind, therefore, arise in the mind by the same necessity as the ideas of things actually existing. Consequently, those who believe that they speak or are silent or do anything else from a free decree of the mind dream with their eyes open.[28]

All things are determined by external causes to exist and operate in a given determinate manner. For instance, a stone receives from the impulsion of an external cause a certain quantity of motion, by virtue of which it continues to move after the impulsion given by the external cause has ceased.—Further conceive that a stone, while continuing in motion, should be capable of thinking and knowing, that it is endeavoring, as far as it can, to continue to move. Such a stone, being conscious merely of its own endeavor and not at all indifferent, would believe itself to be completely free, and would think that it continued in motion solely because of its own wish. This is that human freedom, which all boast that they possess, and which consists solely in the fact that men are conscious of their own desire, but are ignorant of the causes whereby that desire has been determined.—I have thus sufficiently explained my opinion regarding free and constrained necessity, and also regarding so-called human freedom.[29]

However, it is a noteworthy circumstance that Spinoza came to this insight only in his last years (i.e., forties), after having defended the contrary view decisively and vigorously. In the year 1665, when he was still a Cartesian, in his *Cogitata Metaphysica,* he even said—in direct contradiction to the just quoted view concerning Buridan's sophisms—the following: "For were a man instead of the ass placed in such a condition of equilibrium he would be regarded not as a thinking being but as a most stupid ass if he perished of thirst or hunger." [30]

Further on I shall be reporting the same change of view and conversion in two other great men. This proves how difficult and deep down is the correct insight into our problem.

Hume, in his essay *Of Liberty and Necessity,* from which I

---

[28] [*Ibid.,* III, prop. II, end, pp. 133-34.—Tr.]

[29] [Spinoza, *Works* (London: 1912), Vol. II, Letter LXII, pp. 390-91.—Tr.]

[30] [Spinoza, "Cogitata Metaphysica," *The Principles of Descartes' Philosophy* (Chicago: 1905), Vol. II, chap. XII, p. 173, ed. Britan.—Tr.]

have already quoted a passage, writes with the clearest conviction of the necessity of single volitions when the motives are given, and presents this most plainly in his generally intelligible manner. He says: "Thus it appears that the conjunction between motives and voluntary actions is as regular and uniform as that between the cause and effect in any part of nature." And further: "It seems almost impossible, therefore, to engage either in science or action of any kind, without acknowledging the doctrine of necessity and this inference from motives to voluntary actions, from character to conduct." [31]

But no writer has presented the necessity of volitions as extensively and convincingly as Priestley in his work exclusively devoted to this subject, *The Doctrine of Philosophical Necessity*. The understanding of a man who is not convinced by this most clearly and intelligibly written book must be indeed paralyzed by prejudices. To characterize his conclusions I quote several passages:

There is no absurdity more glaring to my understanding, than the notion of philosophical liberty.— Without a miracle, or the intervention of some foreign cause, no volition or action of any man could have been otherwise, than it has been.—Though an inclination or affection of mind be not gravity, it influences me and acts upon me as certainly and necessarily, as this power does upon a stone.—Saying that the will is self-determined, gives no idea at all, or rather implies an absurdity, viz: that a determination, which is an effect, takes place, without any cause at all. For exclusive of every thing that comes under the denomination of motive, there is really nothing at all left, to produce the determination. Let a man use what words he pleases, he can have no more conception how we can sometimes be determined by motives, and sometimes without any motive, than he can have of a scale being sometimes weighed down by weights, and sometimes by a kind of substance that has no weight at all, which, whatever it be in itself, must, with respect to the scale, be nothing.—In proper philosophical language, the motive ought to be called the proper cause

[31] [Hume, *op. cit.*, pp. 89 and 91.—Tr.]

of the action. It is as much so as any thing in nature is the
cause of any thing else.—It will never be in our power to
choose two things, when all the previous circumstances are
the very same.—A man indeed, when he reproaches himself
for any particular action in his passed conduct, may fancy
that, if he was in the same situation again, he would have
acted differently. But this is a mere deception; and if he
examines himself strictly, and takes in all circumstances, he
may be satisfied that, with the same inward disposition of
mind, and with precisely the same view of things, that he
had then, and exclusive of all others, that he has acquired
by reflection since, he could not have acted otherwise than
he did.—In short, there is no choice in the case, but of the
doctrine of necessity or absolute nonsense.[32]

It should be noticed that Priestley underwent the same
change as Spinoza, and also as another great man, soon to be
considered. For Priestley says in the preface to the first edition, "I was not however a ready convert to the doctrine of
necessity. Like Dr. Hartley himself, I gave up my liberty with
great reluctance, and in a long correspondence, which I once
had on the subject, I maintained very strenuously the doctrine
of liberty, and did not at all yield to the arguments then pro-
posed to me." [33]

The third great man to whom the same happened is Voltaire, who reports it himself with the amiability, the charm,
and the naïveté so characteristic of him. In his *Treatise on
Metaphysics* (Chap. VII) he had defended extensively and
vigorously the so-called freedom of the will. But in his book
written more than forty years later, *Le philosophe ignorant*,
he teaches the strict necessity of volitions. Chapter XIII of
this book he concludes thus:

When Archimedes is so deeply engrossed in his problem
that the idea of leaving does not even enter his mind, he is
compelled to remain in his room just as necessarily as he

[32] [Schopenhauer quotes from the second edition of J. Priestley, *Doctrine of Philosophical Necessity* (Birmingham: 1782), pp. xx, 26, 37, 43,
66, 84, 90, 287.—Tr.]
[33] [*Ibid.*, p. xxvii.—Tr.]

would be if one were to lock him up in it. The fates lead
the willing; the unwilling they drive. The fool who thinks
thus has not always thought so; but he was finally forced
to yield.[34]

In the following book Voltaire says:

A ball which hits another ball, a hunting dog which
pursues necessarily and purposely a deer, this deer which
jumps across a wide ditch with no less necessity or purpose
—all this is no more irresistibly determined than are we in
whatever we do.[35]

This uniform conversion to our view of these three so highly
eminent minds surely must startle anyone who undertakes to
attack well-founded truths with that wholly non-pertinent
"but I still can do what I will" of his stupid self-consciousness.

After considering these most immediate predecessors, it
should not surprise us that Kant took the necessity by which
the empirical character is impelled to actions by motives to be
a settled matter, both for him and for others, and did not stop
to prove it anew. In his "Ideas Toward a General History"
he begins in this way: "No matter what concept of the freedom of the will one may make for oneself metaphysically,
still the *appearances* of it, human actions, are determined according to general laws of nature like all other natural events."
In the *Critique of Pure Reason* he says:

Since this empirical character must itself be discovered from
the appearances which are its effect and from the rule to
which experience shows them to conform, it follows that all
the actions of men in the (field of) appearance are determined in conformity with the order of nature, by their
empirical character and by the other causes which cooperate
with that character; and if we could exhaustively investigate all the appearance of men's wills, there would not be
found a single human action which we could not predict
with certainty, and recognize as proceeding necessarily from

34 [Voltaire, *Le Philosophe Ignorant*, chap. XIII.—Tr.]
35 [Voltaire, "Le Principe d'action," chap. XIII, *Mélanges Philo-
sophiques* (Paris: 1781), XX, 255.—Tr.]

its antecedent conditions. So far, then, as regards this empirical character there is no freedom; and yet it is only in
the light of this character that man can be studied—if, that
is to say, we are simply *observing,* and in the manner of
anthropology seeking to institute a physiological investigation into the motive causes of his actions.[36]

In the same work we have:

> If the will be free, this can have a bearing only on the in-
> telligible cause of our volition. For as regards the phe-
> nomena of its outward expressions, that is, of our actions,
> we must account for them—in accordance with a maxim
> which is inviolable, and which is so fundamental that with-
> out it we should not be able to employ reason in any em-
> pirical manner whatsoever—in the same manner as all other
> appearances of nature, namely, in conformity with un-
> changeable laws.[37]

Furthermore, in the *Critique of Practical Reason* Kant says:

> It may be admitted that if it were possible for us to have so
> deep an insight into a man's character as shown both in
> inner and outer actions, that every, even the least, incentive
> to these actions and all external occasions which affect them
> were so known to us that his future conduct could be pre-
> dicted with as great a certainty as the occurrence of a solar
> or lunar eclipse.[38]

But with this he connects his doctrine of the co-existence
of freedom with necessity by means of the distinction between
the intelligible and the empirical character. I shall return to
this view below, since I accept it entirely. Kant expressed it
on two occasions.[39] Anyone who wants to get a thorough understanding of the possibility of unifying human freedom

---

[36] [Immanuel Kant, *Critique of Pure Reason* (London: 1950), p. 474,
trans. Smith.—Tr.]

[37] [*Ibid.,* p. 631.—Tr.]

[38] [Immanuel Kant, *Critique of Practical Reason* (New York: 1956),
pp. 102-03, trans. L. W. Beck.—Tr.]

[39] [Immanuel Kant, *Kritik der reinen Vernunft,* 1st ed. 532-554, 2d ed.
560-582, and according to Schopenhauer, even clearer in the *Critique of
Practical Reason, op. cit.,* pp. 97-107.—Tr.]

with the necessity of actions must read these deeply and thoroughly reasoned passages.

From the achievements of all these noble and honorable predecessors the present treatment of the subject differs primarily on two points. First, guided by the question of this prize essay, I have strictly separated the inner consciousness of the will in the self-consciousness from the outer one, and considered each separately. It was this alone which enabled me to reveal the source of the deception which so irresistibly affects most people. Secondly, I have considered the will in connection with all the rest of nature, something which no one has done before, and solely thanks to which the subject matter could be treated with the thoroughness, methodical penetration, and completeness of which it is capable.

And now a few words about several writers who wrote after Kant but whom I do not consider as my predecessors.

In his "Investigations of Human Freedom," [40] Schelling provided an explicatory paraphrase of Kant's highly important teaching, commended above, about the intelligible and empirical character. Thanks to the vividness of its coloring, this paraphrase can help to make the matter more intelligible for some people than the thorough but dry Kantian presentation. Meanwhile, to honor truth and Kant, I cannot mention it without at the same time uttering a reproof. For in this instance Schelling, while expounding the most important and most admirable, indeed, in my opinion the most profound of all Kant's teachings, does not make clear that the content of what he presents comes from Kant. Instead, he expresses himself in such a way that by far the most readers to whom the content of the prolix and difficult works of the great man are not familiar must suppose that here they are reading Schelling's own ideas. How very successful this intent was I will show by means of only one of many examples.

Even today a young professor of philosophy in Halle, Herr Erdmann, in his book of 1837 entitled *Body and Soul,* says

---

40 [F. W. J. Schelling, *Philosophische Untersuchungen über das Wesen der menschlichen Freiheit und die damit zusammenhängenden Gegenstände* (Leipzig: 1907), p. 479.—Tr.]

the following on p. 101: "Even though Leibnitz, like Schelling in his treatise on freedom, has the soul determine itself before all time, etc." Thus Schelling stands here in respect to Kant in the fortunate position of Amerigo in respect to Columbus: the other's discovery is stamped with his name. But he owes this to his cleverness and not to an accident. For he begins, on p. 476, as follows: "In general, it took idealism to raise the doctrine of freedom to that realm," etc., and then immediately follow the Kantian ideas. So instead of saying here "Kant," as honesty would demand, he cleverly says "idealism." Under this term with multiple meanings everyone will understand the philosophy of Fichte and Schelling's early, Fichtean philosophy, and not Kant's doctrine, since the latter had protested against calling his philosophy idealism, and had even added to the second edition of the *Critique of Pure Reason* a "Refutation of Idealism." [41] Then, on the next page Schelling very shrewdly mentions, in a parenthetical phrase, the "Kantian concept," in order namely to pacify those who already know that it is Kantian riches which one is displaying with such pomp as one's own goods. But then on p. 484 it is written, in defiance of all truth and justice, that Kant did *not* rise to the height of this view in his theory, etc., whereas everyone can see clearly from the immortal passages of Kant which I have recommended above for re-reading that precisely this view originally belongs to him alone, and even a thousand such heads as Fichte's and Schelling's would never have been capable of grasping this without him.

Since I had to speak here of Schelling's treatise I could not remain silent on this point. By restoring to Kant that which indisputably belongs to him alone I have merely fulfilled my duty toward that great teacher of mankind who, along with Goethe, is all by himself the just pride of the German nation —especially at a time when Goethe's words, "Children are the masters of the road," [42] ring true indeed. By the way, in the

---

[41] [Kant, *Critique of Pure Reason, op. cit.,* p. 244ff.—Tr.]

[42] [Goethe, "Parabolisch," "das Knabenvolk ist Herr der Bahn."—Tr.]

same treatise Schelling hesitated just as little to appropriate the ideas and even the words of Jakob Boehme, without betraying his source.

Besides this paraphrase of Kant's thoughts, those "Investigations of Freedom" contain nothing that could serve to provide us with new or basic elucidations of them. This is made evident at the very outset in the definition: he says freedom is "a capacity for good and evil." For the catechism such a definition may be of some use, but in philosophy nothing is said by it and, consequently, nothing can be done with it. For good and evil are far from being simple concepts (*notiones simplices*) which, clear in themselves, require no explanation, establishment, and foundation. All in all, only a small part of that treatise is concerned with freedom; its main content is rather an extended report about a God with whom the author reveals an intimate familiarity, since he even describes for us his origination. It is only a pity that he does not say, even in a single word, how he arrived at this familiarity. The beginning of the treatise consists of a web of sophisms, whose shallowness will be recognized by anyone who is not intimidated by the audacity of the tone.

Since that time and as a result of this and similar productions, "intellectual contemplation" and "absolute thinking" have replaced distinct concepts and honest searching in German philosophy. Bluffing, confounding, mystification, scattering sand in the reader's eyes by all sorts of tricks—have become the method. Instead of insight, selfish purpose everywhere guides the discourse. Thanks to all this, philosophy, if one still wants to call it that, has had to sink lower and lower, until it finally reached the lowest level of abasement in the ministerial creature Hegel. This man, in order to smother again the freedom of thought which Kant had struggled for and won, made of philosophy—the daughter of reason and the future mother of truth—a tool of state aims, obscurantism, and Protestant Jesuitism. But in order to cover up the disgrace and at the same time to bring about the greatest possible stupefaction of minds, he drew over it a cloak of the emptiest word rubbish and silliest gallimathias that have ever been heard outside the insane asylum.

In England and France, philosophy by and large still stands where Locke and Condillac left it. Maine de Biran, called by his publisher Cousin "the leading French metaphysician of my time," is a fanatical follower of the *liberum arbitrium indifferentiae* in his *New Considerations of Physics and Morality,* published in 1834, and regards it as completely obvious. Some of the recent German philosophical scribes do not proceed any differently; the *liberum arbitrium indifferentiae,* under the name of "moral freedom," appears in their writings as a matter of course, just as if all the above-mentioned great men had never existed. They declare the freedom of the will to be immediately given in the self-consciousness and therefore so unshakably established that all arguments against it could be nothing but sophisms. This exalted confidence stems only from the fact that the good fellows don't even know what freedom of the will is and means, and in their innocence understand by it no more than the mastery of the will over the parts of the body, which we analyzed in the second section. But this was never doubted by any reasonable person and is expressed precisely by that notion "I can do what I will." They think quite honestly that this is the freedom of the will and boast that it is beyond any possible doubt. This is precisely the state of innocence into which, after so many great predecessors, German thought has been set back by the Hegelian philosophy. To the people of this kind one certainly could call out:

> Are ye not like the women, who for ever
> Only recur to their first word, although
> One has been talking reason by the hour? [43]

---

[43] [Schiller, *The Death of Wallenstein,* Act II, Scene 3, trans. Churchill and Martin.

> Seid ihr nicht wie die Weiber, die beständig
> Zurück nur kommen auf ihr erstes Wort,
> Wenn man Vernunft gesprochen stundenlang?

—Tr.]

Still in some of them the above-indicated theological motives may be secretly at work.

And then again there are the medical, zoological, historical, political, and literary writers of our times—how very gladly they grasp every opportunity to mention the "freedom of man" and the "moral freedom"! They feel important when they say this. Of course they do not enter into an explanation of it. But if one were allowed to examine them, one would find that they mean by this either nothing at all or our old, honest, well-known *liberum arbitrium indifferentiae,* no matter in what elegant turns of phrase they might clothe it. It will probably never be possible to convince the masses of the invalidity of this concept, but at least scholars should beware of speaking about it with so much innocence. Hence too one can find among them some timid fellows who, very amusingly, no longer dare to speak of the freedom of the will, but, in order to make it elegant, say instead "freedom of the spirit" and hope to slink through in this fashion. But fortunately I am in a position to inform the reader, who now looks at me questioningly, what they think when they say this. Nothing, absolutely nothing. It is no more than, in keeping with the good German fashion and style, an indefinite expression, indeed, an expression which actually says nothing at all and which merely provides a way out, so much coveted by their emptiness and cowardice.

The word "spirit"—really a metaphorical term—always designates the *intellectual* capacities, in contrast to the will. But these are not supposed to be free at all in their operation, but are said to obey, conform, and be subject first to the rules of logic and then to the given object of their cognition, in order that they may comprehend clearly, that is, objectively— and that it could never be said: will replaces reason.[44] In general, this "spirit," which hangs around everywhere in contemporary German literature, is a thoroughly suspicious fellow who therefore should be asked for his credentials wherever he is encountered. His most frequent occupation is

[44] [Juvenal, VI, 223.—Tr.]

to serves as the mask of poverty of thought, which is combined with cowardice. Incidentally, the word *Geist* ("spirit") is related, as is well known, to the word "gas" which, stemming from the Arabic and from alchemy, stands for "fog" or "air," just as *spiritus* and *pneuma*, or *animus* related to *anemos*, meaning "breath."

So this is the way things stand with respect to our topic in the philosophical and in all the learned world, after all that the cited great minds have taught about it. This confirms again not only that nature has at all times produced very few real thinkers, as rare exceptions, but also that these few have themselves existed only for very few. Precisely for this reason, folly and error continue their reign.

In connection with a moral subject, the testimony of the great poets also has weight. What they say is not a result of systematic investigation; nevertheless, human nature is open to their penetrating gaze. Consequently, their assertions hit immediately upon the truth. In Shakespeare's *Measure for Measure* Isabella asks mercy of the vice-regent Angelo for her brother, who is sentenced to death:

> *Angelo:* I will not do it.
> *Isab.:* But can you if you would?
> *Angelo:* Look, what I *will* not, that I *cannot* do.[45]

In *Twelfth Night* it is said:

> Fate show thy force, ourselves we do not owe,
> What is decree'd must be, and be this so.[46]

Also Walter Scott, that great judge and painter of the human heart and of its most secret stirrings, brought this deep-seated truth clearly to light in his *St. Ronan's Well*, Vol. 3, chap. VI. He presents a dying, repentant sinner who tries on her deathbed to ease her uneasy conscience by confessions. In the midst of them he has her say:

> Go, and leave me to my fate; I am the most detestable wretch, that ever liv'd,—detestable to myself, worst of all;

[45] [William Shakespeare, *Measure for Measure*, Act II, Scene 2.—Tr.]
[46] [William Shakespeare, *Twelfth Night*, Act I, Scene 5.—Tr.]

because even in my penitence there is a secret whisper that tells me, that were I as I have been, I would again act over all the wickedness I have done, and much worse. Oh! for Heaven's assistance, to crush the wicked thought!

The following fact, parallel to this poetic illustration, substantiates it and at the same time confirms most forcefully the doctrine of the constancy of character. It was reprinted from the French newspaper *La Presse* in the [London] *Times* of July 2, 1845, from which I translate it. The heading is as follows: "Military Execution in Oran."

On March 24th the Spaniard Anguilar, alias Gomez, had been sentenced to death. The day before the execution he said in conversation with his jailer, I am not as guilty as they have represented me. I am accused of committing 30 murders, whereas I have committed only 26. From childhood on I had a thirst for blood; when I was seven and a half years old I stabbed a child to death. I have murdered a pregnant woman, and at a later time a Spanish officer, as a result of which act I saw myself compelled to flee Spain. I fled to France, where I committed two crimes before entering the Foreign Legion. Among all my crimes I regret most of all the following. In the year 1841, while at the head of my company, I took prisoner a deputy general-commissar, who was escorted by a sergeant, a corporal, and seven men. I had them all beheaded. The death of these people weighs heavily on me; I see them in my dreams, and tomorrow I shall see them in the soldiers who are ordered to shoot me. Nevertheless, if I should get my freedom again, I would murder still more people.

The following passage in Goethe's *Iphigenia* also belongs here:

> *Arkas:* Thou didst not heed this loyal friend's advice.
> *Iphigenia:* Gladly I did what I had power to do.
> *Arkas:* There still is time for thee to change thy mind.
> *Iphigenia:* Once and for all, that's not within our power.[47]

47 [Act IV, Scene 2. Translation by B. Q. Morgan.

> *Arkas:* Denn du hast nicht der Treue Rat geachtet.
> *Iphigenie:* Was ich vermochte, hab' ich gern getan.
> *Arkas:* Noch änderst du den Sinn zur rechten Zeit.
> *Iphigenie:* Das steht nun einmal nicht in unsrer Macht.—Tr.]

A famous passage in Schiller's *Wallenstein's Tod* likewise expresses our basic truth:

> Know that the human being's thoughts and deeds
> Are not like ocean billows, blindly swinging.
> His inner world, his microcosmos, breeds
> Them in the shaft profound whence they keep springing.
> One can predict them like the fruit of a tree;
> No juggling chance can alter truth and fact.
> Once I've explored a man's identity,
> I also know his will and how he'll act.[48]

48 [Act II, Scene 3. Translation by B. Q. Morgan.

> Des Menschen Taten und Gedanken, wisst,
> Sind nicht wie Meeres blind bewegte Wellen.
> Die inn're Welt, sein Mikrokosmus, ist
> Der tiefe Schacht, aus dem sie ewig quellen.
> Sie sind notwendig wie des Baumes Frucht,
> Sie kann der Zufall gaukelnd nicht verwandeln.
> Hab' ich des Menschen Kern erst untersucht,
> So weiss ich auch sein Wollen und sein Handeln.—Tr.]

CONCLUSION AND A HIGHER VIEW

I was glad to recall to the reader all those glorious, poetical as well as philosophical, predecessors who stood for the truth which I also defend. However, it is not authorities but reasons that constitute the philosopher's weapon. Consequently, in defending my case I relied on reasons alone and yet hope to have supplied enough evidence to justify me fully in drawing the conclusion *a non posse ad non esse* (from impossibility to non-existence). Thus, while in the above investigation of the self-consciousness the denial of the question of the Royal Society could be based on direct and factual, hence a posteriori evidence, it is now justified also immediately and a priori, since what does not exist at all cannot have in the self-consciousness any data from which it could be proved.

The truth which I defend may be one of those to which the preconceived opinions of the short-sighted masses are opposed. Indeed, it may be offensive to the weak and the ignorant. But this must not keep me from presenting it without circumlocutions and without reserve, seeing that I am not talking here to the populace but to an enlightened Academy, which has posed its very timely question not for the sake of strengthening prejudice, but to honor the truth. Moreover, as long as it is a matter of establishing and confirming the truth, the honest seeker will always look to its grounds alone and not to its consequences. The time for that will come when the truth itself is established. Unconcerned about the consequences, we are only to examine our grounds, without first asking whether a recognized truth is or is not in harmony with the system of our other convictions. This is what Kant recommends, whose words I cannot refrain from repeating here:

[This strengthens] the maxim, already known and recommended by others, that in every scientific investigation we should unswervingly pursue our course with all possible accuracy and candor without attending to any extraneous difficulties it might involve, carrying out as far as we can our investigation by itself honestly and completely. Frequent observation has convinced me that once one has seen through such business, that which, when half-finished, appeared very dubious in view of extraneous theories is at last found to be in an unexpected way completely harmonious with that which had been discovered separately without the least regard for them, provided this dubiousness is left out of sight for a while and only the business at hand is attended to until it is finished. Writers would save themselves many errors and much labor lost (because spent on delusions) if they could only resolve to go to work with a little more ingenuousness.[1]

Our metaphysical knowledge in general is still infinitely far from being so certain that one could afford to reject any thoroughly proper truth simply because its consequences do not fit in with that knowledge. It is rather the case that every attained and established truth is conquered territory in the realm of problems of knowledge in general. As such it is a firm point at which we may apply the lever which will move other loads and from which, in favorable cases, one may indeed soar all at once to a higher view of the whole than one had hitherto. For the concatenation of the truths in every area of knowledge is so great that one who has gained a completely firm possession of a single truth may possibly hope to conquer the whole from there. As in a difficult algebraic problem a single positively-given magnitude is of inestimable value because it makes the solution possible, so in the most difficult of all human problems, which is metaphysics, such an inestimable datum is the certain knowledge, proved a priori and a posteriori, of the strict necessity with which acts follow from a given character and given motives. From this datum alone, using it as a starting point, we can arrive at the solution of the entire problem. Hence everything for which a firm,

[1] [Kant, *Critique of Practical Reason*, p. 110.—Tr.]

scientific verification cannot be produced must yield to such a well-founded truth, if it stands in its way, and not the other way around. And such a truth must by no means be subjected to accommodations and limitations in order to be harmonized with unproved and perhaps erroneous assertions.

Let me make still another general remark. A retrospect on our result occasions the observation that in respect to the two problems—already designated in the previous section as the deepest problems of modern philosophy (although not clearly apprehended by the ancients), namely, the problem of the freedom of the will and the problem of the relation between the ideal and the real—the healthy but untutored mind is not only incompetent, but even has a decided natural tendency to error. To free it of this error a highly developed philosophy is required. For in matters concerning cognition it is really natural for that mind to attribute altogether too much to the object. Therefore it took Locke and Kant to show how much of this arises from the subject. With respect to the will on the other hand, such a mind has the opposite tendency, to attribute too little to the object and too much to the subject. It makes the willing proceed exclusively from the subject, without taking proper account of the factor located in the object, that is, of the motives which really determine the entire individual character of actions. Only the general and essential aspect of actions, namely, their basic moral character, proceeds from the subject. However, such a perversity in speculative investigations, natural to the mind, should not surprise us, for originally the mind is designed only for practical and by no means for speculative purposes.

The result of our preceding exposition was to recognize the complete annulment of all freedom of human action and its thorough-going subjection to the strictest necessity. But it is precisely by this route that we are now led to the point where we shall be able to grasp the true moral freedom, which is of a higher sort.

For there is another fact of consciousness which until now I have left completely aside in order not to interfere with the process of my investigation. This is the wholly clear and certain feeling of the *responsibility* for what we do, of the accountability for our actions, which rests on the unshakable certainty that we ourselves are the doers of our deeds. By virtue of this consciousness it will never enter the head of even the one who is fully convinced of the necessity (set forth above) with which our actions take place to make this necessity excuse a transgression and to shift the blame from himself to the motives, arguing that when they entered in the act was inevitable. For he sees very clearly that this necessity has a subjective condition, and that objectively, that is, under the existing circumstances, hence under the influence of the motives which determined him, a quite different action, indeed, an action exactly opposite to the one he performed, was quite possible and could have happened, *if only he had been another*—this alone kept him from doing something else. To him, because he is this man and no other, because he has such and such a character, no different action was of course possible; but in itself, i.e., objectively, it *was* possible. So the responsibility of which he is conscious falls upon the act only provisionally and ostensibly, but basically it falls upon *his character*—for this he feels responsible. And it is for his character that the others also make him responsible; their verdict immediately abandons the act in order to establish the characteristics of the agent: "he is a bad man, a villain," or "he is a rascal," or "he is a small, false, despicable soul"—thus runs their verdict, and their reproaches fall back on his character. The act, together with motive, is considered in this connection only as a witness to the agent's character, but is nevertheless regarded as a sure symptom of the latter, through which it is irrevocably and forever established.

Aristotle says therefore quite correctly: "Hence it is only when a man has already done something that we bestow *encomiums* upon him. Yet the actual deeds are evidence of the doer's character: even if a man has not actually done a given good thing, we shall bestow *praise* on him, if we are sure that he is the sort of man who *would* do it." [2] So hate, abhorrence, and contempt do not descend on the transitory act, but on the persisting characteristics of the agent, that is, on the character from which they issued. This explains why in all languages the epithets of moral badness, the abusive names which describe it, are predicates of men rather than of their actions. They are attached to the character, and the character must bear the guilt of which it has been convicted merely on the strength of its acts.

Where guilt lies, there responsibility must lie also, and since the latter is the only datum which entitles us to infer moral freedom, freedom must also have the same location, namely, in the character of man; the more so since we convinced ourselves sufficiently that it cannot be found immediately in individual actions, which take place with strict necessity when the character is assumed. But character, as was shown in the third section, is inborn and unchangeable.

Let us now view somewhat more closely the freedom interpreted in this sense, the only sense for which the data are before us, in order, having inferred it from a fact of consciousness and found its location, to grasp it philosophically too, as far as that may be possible.

In the third section the result reached was that every action of a man is the product of two factors: his character along with a motive. This by no means signifies something which lies midway, a compromise as it were, between the motive and the character. No, it does full justice to both, as, in accordance with its total possibility, it rests on both at the same time in this way: the acting motive encounters this particular character, and this character is determinable by such a motive. The character is the empirically recognized, persistent, and unchangeable nature of an individual will. Since this character is just as necessary a factor of each action as is the motive, this fact explains the feeling that our acts proceed from ourselves, or explains that "I will" which accompanies all our

2 [Aristotle, *Rhetoric*, I, 9, 1367b, 31.—Tr.]

actions and by virtue of which everyone must recognize them as *his* actions, for which he therefore feels morally responsible. But this is again that "I will, and will always only that which I will"—encountered above in the examination of the self-consciousness—which misleads the untutored understanding into maintaining stubbornly an absolute freedom of commission and omission, a *liberum arbitrium indifferentiae*. However, this is nothing more than the consciousness of the second factor of the action, which by itself would be quite incapable of bringing it about and which, on the other hand, is just as incapable of refraining from it after a motive appears. But only as it is thus put into action does it reveal its own nature to the cognitive faculty. This faculty, essentially directed outward, not inward, actually learns the nature of its own will only from its actions, empirically. What one calls conscience is really this closer and progressively more intimate acquaintance. For just this reason conscience makes itself heard directly only after the action. Prior to that it speaks at most only indirectly as it deliberates about a future occurrence by means of reflection and review of similar cases on which it has already declared itself.

This is the place for a reminder of the illustration already mentioned in the previous section. It was Kant's presentation of the relation between the empirical and the intelligible character and thereby of the possibility of uniting freedom with necessity. It is one of the most beautiful and profound ideas brought forth by that great mind, or indeed by men at any time. I need only to refer to it, because to repeat it here would be a superfluous prolixity. But it is only with its help that it is possible to comprehend, insofar as human powers can, how the strict necessity of our actions nevertheless coexists with that freedom to which the feeling of responsibility testifies and by virtue of which we are the agents of our acts, these actions being morally ascribable to us.

That relation of the empirical to the intelligible character demonstrated by Kant rests entirely on that which constitutes the basic feature of his whole philosophy, namely, on the distinction between appearance and thing-in-itself. As for him the complete empirical reality of the world of experience co-exists with its transcendental ideality, so the strict empirical necessity of action coexists with its transcendental freedom. For the empirical character, like the whole man, is a mere appearance as an object of experience, and hence bound to the forms of all appearance—time, space, and causality—and subject to their laws. On the other hand, the condition and the basis of this whole appearance—which as a thing-in-itself is independent of these forms and therefore not subject to time distinctions but is persistent and unchangeable—is his intelligible character, i.e., his will as thing-in-itself. It is to the will in this capacity that freedom, and to be sure even absolute freedom, that is, independence of the law of causality (as a mere form of appearances), properly belongs.

This freedom, however, is transcendental, i.e., it does not occur in appearance. It is present only insofar as we abstract from the appearance and from all its forms in order to reach that which, since it is outside of all time, must be thought of as the inner being of man-in-himself. By virtue of this freedom all acts of man are of his own making, no matter how necessarily they proceed from the empirical character when it encounters the motives. This is so because the empirical character is only the appearance of the intelligible character, in our cognitive faculty as bound to time, space, and causality—i.e., the manner in which the essence-in-itself of our own self presents itself to this faculty. Accordingly, the will is of course free, but only in itself and outside of appearance. In appearance, on the contrary, it presents itself already with a definite character, with which all of its actions are in conformity and therefore, when further determined by the supervening motives, must turn out thus and not otherwise.

As can easily be seen, this road leads to the view that we must no longer seek the work of our freedom in our individual actions, as the general opinion does, but in the whole being and essence (*existentia et essentia*) of the man himself. This must be thought of as his free act, which only presents itself to the cognitive faculty as linked to time, space, and causality in a multiplicity and variety of actions. But precisely because of the original unity of that which manifests itself in them, all actions must have exactly the same character and therefore appear as strictly necessitated in each case by the motives by which they are called forth and determined in detail. Accordingly, for the world of experience the *operari sequitur esse* is firmly established without exception. Everything acts according to its nature, and its acts as they respond to causes make this nature known. Every man acts according to what he is, and the action, which is accordingly necessary in each case, is determined solely by the motives in the individual case.

The freedom which therefore cannot be encountered in the *operari* must lie in the *esse*. It has been a fundamental error of all ages, an unwarranted inversion (hysteron-proteron), to attribute necessity to the *esse* and freedom to the *operari*. The converse is true: freedom lies in the *esse* alone, but the *operari* follows necessarily from it and the motives. *From what we do we know what we are.* On this, and not on the presumed *liberum arbitrium indifferentiae,* rests the consciousness of responsibility and the moral tendency of life. Everything depends on what one is; what he does will follow therefrom of itself, as a necessary corollary. The consciousness of self-determination and originality which undeniably accompanies all our acts, and by virtue of which they are *our* acts, is therefore not deceptive, in spite of their dependence on motives. But its true content reaches further than the acts and begins higher up. In truth it includes our being and essence itself, from which all acts proceed necessarily when motives arise. In this sense that consciousness of self-determination and originality, as well as the consciousness of responsibility accompanying our actions, can be compared to a hand which points to an object more remote than the one nearer by to which it seems to be pointing.

In a word: man does at all times only what he wills, and yet he does this necessarily. But this is due to the fact that he already *is* what he wills. For from that which he *is*, there follows of necessity everything that he, at any time, *does.* If we consider his behavior objectively, i.e., from the outside, we shall be bound to recognize that, like the behavior of every natural being, it must be subject to the law of causality in all its severity. Subjectively, however, everyone feels that he always does only what he wills. But this merely means that his activity is a pure expression of his very own being. Every natural being, even the lowest, would feel the same, if it *could* feel.

Consequently, my exposition does not eliminate freedom. It merely moves it out, namely, out of the area of simple actions, where it demonstrably cannot be found, up to a region which lies higher, but is not so easily accessible to our knowledge. In other words, freedom is transcendental. And this is also the sense in which I should like to interpret the statement of Malebranche,[3] *la liberté est un mystère,* under whose aegis the present dissertation has attempted to solve the problem set by the Royal Society.

[3] [According to Deussen, Schopenhauer's editor, Malebranche did not use exactly these words, but nevertheless expressed the same idea in one of his writings, "Entretiens sur la métaphysique," IV, chap. XVI.–Tr.]

APPENDIX

SUPPLEMENTARY TO THE FIRST CHAPTER

In the very beginning I introduced a division of freedom into physical, intellectual, and moral freedom. The first and the last have been discussed, and now I still have to examine the second. This is to be done merely for the sake of completeness, hence very briefly.

The intellect, or the cognitive faculty, is the medium of motives. Through this medium they act on the will, which is the real essence of man. Only insofar as this medium of motives is in a normal state, performs its function correctly, and hence puts before the choosing will the motives undistorted, as they are in the real external world, can this will decide according to its nature, that is, according to the man's individual character. In such a case it can express itself unconstrained, in accordance with its own essence. The man is then *intellectually* free, that is, his actions are the pure result of the reaction of his will to motives which are present to him in the external world as they are to others. Accordingly, actions must be charged up to him, both morally and legally.

This intellectual freedom is eliminated either when the medium of the motives—the cognitive faculty—is permanently or temporarily disarranged, or when in an individual case external circumstances falsify the comprehension of the motives. The former happens in madness, delirium, paroxysm, and somnolence, the latter in the case of definite and innocent error, for instance, when a man fills a glass with poison instead of medicine, or when he mistakes a servant entering at night for a burglar and shoots him, etc. For in both cases the motives are falsified and because of this the will cannot decide as it would decide, had the intellect correctly reported to it the actual circumstances. Crimes committed under such circumstances are therefore not legally punishable. For the laws proceed from the correct assumption that the will is not morally free—in which case one could not guide it—but is subject to constraint by motives. Accordingly, by threat of punishment the laws want to confront all motives to crime with stronger countermotives. A criminal code is nothing but a list of countermotives to criminal actions. But if the intellect, through which these countermotives have to act, was incapable of grasping them and holding them up to the will, then their action was impossible: they did not exist for that will. It is as when one finds out that one of the wires required to move a machine is broken. Consequently, in such cases the guilt is transferred to the intellect. Intellect, however, is not subject to punishment; laws, as well as morality, have to do only with the will. It alone is the authentic man, while the intellect is merely its organ, its antennae to the outside, i.e., the medium for the action of motives upon it.

Just as little are such acts to be morally imputed. For they are not a feature of a man's character. Either he did something different from what he believed himself to be doing, or he was incapable of thinking of that which should have kept him from doing it, i.e., he was incapable of admitting countermotives. This is analogous to what may happen in investigating the chemical composition of a substance. A substance is exposed to the influence of several reagents in order to find out to which it has the strongest affinity. If after the completion of the experiment one should find that accidentally one of the reagents could not act at all, the experiment is invalid.

Intellectual freedom, which in the above instance we regarded as completely eliminated, sometimes may be merely diminished, or eliminated only to some extent. This happens especially in passion and in intoxication. Passion is the sudden, violent excitation of the will by means of an idea which penetrates from the outside and becomes a motive. This idea possesses such a vivacity that it obscures all others which could work against it as countermotives and keeps them from entering clearly into consciousness. While the latter are for the most part only of an abstract nature, i.e., mere thoughts, the former idea is something perceptibly actual. Consequently the countermotives do not get a chance to shoot, so to speak, and hence we do not have what in English is called fair play; the act has occurred before they could oppose it. It is as if in a duel one participant fired before the signal was given.

Accordingly, in this case too, the legal and the moral responsibility, depending on the circumstances, is more or less, but always in part, eliminated. In England, a murder committed in great precipitancy and without the slightest deliberation, or in the most violent, suddenly provoked anger, is called manslaughter and only lightly punished, indeed, sometimes not at all.

Intoxication is a condition which disposes toward passions by heightening the liveliness of perceptual ideas, but, on the other hand, weakening the power to think *in abstracto*, at the same time increasing the energy of the will. Instead of being responsible for acts we are responsible for the intoxication itself. Hence intoxication is not legally excused, even though in this case intellectual freedom is partly eliminated.

Aristotle speaks, although very briefly and insufficiently, of this intellectual freedom, of the "voluntary and involuntary with respect to reason," in *Ethica Eudemia* (II, chap. VII and IX), and somewhat more extensively in *Nicomachean Ethics* (III, 2). This freedom is referred to when forensic medicine and criminal justice ask whether a criminal was in a state of freedom and hence accountable.

In general, then, all those crimes are to be regarded as committed in the absence of intellectual freedom in which the man either did not know what he was doing or was simply not capable of considering that which should have kept him from doing it, namely, the consequences of the act. Accordingly, in such cases he is not to be punished.

Those who think that no criminal should be punished, simply because moral freedom does not exist and because, as a consequence, all actions of a given man are inevitable, start out from a false view of punishment, namely, that it is a visitation inflicted upon the crime for its own sake, a repayment of evil with evil on moral grounds. This, however, in spite of the fact that Kant taught it, would be absurd, useless, and completely unjustified. For how could a man be empowered to set himself up as an absolute moral judge of another, and as such to torment him because of his sins! Rather, the aim of the law, i.e., of the threat of punishment, is to act as a countermotive to crimes not yet committed. If in a given case the law fails in this effect, still it must be carried out, for otherwise it would also fail in all future cases. The criminal on his part suffers punishment in this case really as a consequence of his moral nature, which in combination with the circumstances (the motives) and his intellect (which falsely promised him the hope of escaping punishment) inevitably brought about the act. In this case injustice could be done to him only if his moral character were not of his own making, not his act as intelligible being, but the work of another.

The same relation of the act to its consequences holds when the consequences of his vicious behavior take place not in accordance with human but with natural laws, e.g., when wretched dissipations bring about terrible diseases, or when a man in attempting a burglary comes to grief accidentally, as in the case of a man who upon breaking into a pigpen at night in order to abduct its usual occupant encountered instead, approaching him with open arms, a bear, whose keeper had found shelter for the night in that inn.